Draketown

Tragedy

Elaine Bolden Bailey

and

Patricia Lamar Mullinax

Based on True Events

Lillium Press

Books by Elaine Bolden Bailey:

Pompadour and Pearls: a Patchwork of Poetry

Buttermilk Clouds

Tracks

Explosion in Villa Rica

Draketown Tragedy

Collaboration with John Bailey on his book:

The History of Dark Corner Campbell County, Georgia

Hart Town Environs

Co-authored with John B. Bailey

Books by Patricia Lamar Mullinax:

Draketown Tragedy

Collaborated with Steve Mullinax on his books:

In the Line of Fire

Confederate Belt Buckles and Plates

Draketown

Tragedy

Draketown Tragedy

Copyright © 2015 by Elaine Bolden Bailey & Patricia Lamar Mullinax
Second Printing 2023

This historical novel is inspired by true events.
Some of the names have been changed to protect the
families of those arrested and released or acquitted.

Website: lilliumpress.net by Fred Finch Graphics;
www.fredricfinch.com
Editor: Richard F. Argo
ISBN: 978-0-9628023-4-8

Front cover photo courtesy: Patricia Mullinax Pope
Back cover photo: Hazel Barnes
Cover design: Fred Finch Graphics

Page 156: Six-year-old, Lorene, center, released the drape to
unveil the monument to her mother, who was killed by moonshiners.
The Ku Klux Klan purchased and erected the monument
and were in charge of the unveiling ceremony.

Back Cover: Photo of Alice Stewart on the side of the monument
erected in her memory.

⚜ Lillium Press

This book is dedicated to

the family of

Alice "Wildie" Adams Stewart.

The Boll Weevil Song

1. The boll weevil's a little black bug,
That came from Mexico, they say,
He came all the way to Texas,
Looking for a place to stay,
Just looking for a home.

2. The first time I saw the boll weevil,
He was flying through the air.
The next time I saw the boll weevil,
His whole family was flying there.
They were looking for a home.

3. The farmer took the boll weevil,
And he put him in the sun.
The weevil said, "This is mighty hot,
But I'll stand it if I can,
This will be my home."

4. The farmer took the boll weevil,
Threw him in a fire's blaze.
The boll weevil said to the farmer
"You can't count my days.
This will be my home."

4. The farmer asked the weevil:
"What makes your head so red?"
The weevil said to the farmer,
"It's a wonder I'm not dead,
I'm looking for a home."

5. The farmer took the boll weevil,
Sprayed him with yellow dust;
The boll weevil said to the farmer:
"Why'd you raise this awful fuss?
All I need's a family home."

7. The boll weevil told the farmer:
"You'd better leave me alone;
I want to eat all your cotton,
Then I'll start on your corn,
I have to have a home."

8. The merchants got half the cotton,
The boll weevil got the rest.
He left the poor farmer's wife
Only one old cotton dress,
Finally weevil's got a home.

9. The farmer told the merchant:
"We're in an awful fix:
The boll weevil ate the cotton
And left us only sticks,
We're afraid we'll loose our home."

10. The farmer told the merchant:
"We made only one bale,
Before we let you have it,
We'd sooner go to jail,
We have to keep our home."

11. The master told the mistress:
"What do you think of that?
The boll weevil's made a nest
In my best Sunday hat,
Can't lose our family home."

12. "And if anybody should ask you
Who it was that made this song,
Just tell them it's the farmer
In overalls walking the road-long,
Who has lost his home."

Contents

Prologue p. 9

Introduction p. 15

1. New Itinerate Preacher p. 19

2. Bad Times p. 33

3. Why Stewart Hates Alcohol p. 51

4. Warfare on Bootleggers p. 67

5. Spirits Collide p. 91

6. Two Night-Riders Wounded p. 99

7. The Posse p. 105

8. The Community & State Reacts p. 123

9. Lies and Alibis p. 135

10. Thunderball Over Draketown p. 155

11. Moonshiners Without a Still p. 163

12. A Silent Movie—*The Raiding Parson* p. 171

13. The Rest of the Story p. 183

Bibliography p. 190

Excerpts from The Haralson County Tribune 1922-1925.

Almost any town can support from three to five citizens who wear three-dollar hats on thirty-cent heads. * Even when a Buchanan woman knows her husband's lying, she keeps right on asking questions. * Relatives are people who wonder how you and your family manage to keep from starving to death. * Doctors are recommending onions as a cure for indigestion. But as yet they haven't found anything to cure onions.

We know a Buchanan man who says he doesn't like two-pant suits because it makes him uncomfortable to wear both pairs at a time. * A woman boiled water all night because a convict escaped. * Nothing can equal the sneer a bald-headed man has for the Willieboy with his hair hanging down in his eyes.

They say that President Coolidge never smiles. Wonder if he has ever seen a pair of those bell bottomed pants? * The fireless cooker (an electric stove) may be all right, but it's not as comfortable as the old kitchen stove when you back up to it on a cold day. * One of the hardest things to find in Buchanan is a friend who isn't hard up at the same time you are.

Some states enjoy ridiculing the senators from other states. It helps them to forget the shortcoming of their own. * My wife and I had words, I didn't get to use mine. * The worst beaten I ever got was for puttin' cayenne pepper in my mother's snuff.

A few chickens of well-selected breed can do much toward lifting the mortgage from the old farm. * You should never judge another person until you walk his daily path and deal with the ups and downs of his life. * Sometimes one's devotion to his Bible can be as bad as another mans devotion to his whisky. * Some men are so focused on the next world, they forget to enjoy their life in this world.

* You could see "lost cause" stamped on every face. * Georgia voted out whisky in 1907. * Prohibition began in the United States on January 17, 1920 at 12.01 a.m. * Will Rodgers said, "If you think this country ain't dry, just watch 'em vote: if you think this country ain't wet, just watch 'em drink. You see, when they vote, it's counted, but when they drink, it ain't" * From almost the dawn of history men have made laws to restrict the sale and use of liquor and men have found ways to get around its laws.

Prologue

I was ten years old, in the summer of 1957, when I first saw the fifteen-foot white marble obelisk gleaming in the morning sun; I studied it long and hard and remember the sphere on top. I was riding with my daddy, a substitute mail carrier. My brother, Ronnie, and I thought our daddy the greatest: boy scout leader, WWII veteran, deacon in the church. Now we got to ride with him on the Draketown mail route. We traveled the route slowly, putting mail in the boxes, when suddenly the monument appeared out of nowhere. It looked a 100 feet tall to my 10-year-old eyes. I guessed it was for a WWII veteran. I never forgot it.

Thirty years later, a small, lovely lady walked into the beauty shop where I worked. "Can you work a miracle on this mess of hair?" She laughed and sat down in my chair in front of the mirror. We began to talk and "fix" her hair. Thus began a five-year friendship with my customer, Arreda Bingham Denton, who would reveal many stories about Draketown and the monument.

After Arreda died in 1994, I carried her stories in my head for another twenty years. This book is the fruition of my dream to "write it all down."
Trisha Mullinax

My friend Trisha told me about wanting to record the events in the 1920s Draketown. She told me Arreda's stories. We decided to write this book together. For the next two years, we researched and collected photos. We recorded one or two interviews a week or visited an achieve or library.
Elaine Bailey

Searching for the truth and putting this story together was like finding a ninety-year-old antique trunk in a dusty attic. First we picked the lock to reveal newspapers that crumpled to the touch and faded photographs of barely recognizable subjects. Yellowed documents taught us the sermons and songs of the day and the habits and dress of the 1920s. We saw an old typewriters and desk and a ninety-year-old death certificate. We trampled through tall grass of ancient cemeteries and stood in reverence in the very courthouse where the trials were held. We searched the internet for a 1926 silent movie. We shuffled and waved metal detectors and dug in the dirt of Draketown on a 90 degree June day, looking for the eight bullets fired—to no avail.

Together we researched archives, libraries and courthouses: the Federal Archives in Morrow, Emory University Pitts Theology Library, the Bremen Public Library, Rome Floyd County Library, Rockmart City Public Library, the Tallapoosa Public Library, the Buchanan Old Courthouse Library and the Buchanan Courthouse. We found a few old newspapers and were devastated to learn no court records existed; after fifty years, it is legal to destroy court records and that is what happened in the ninety years since the trials associated with this tragedy.

Our search took us to on-line sites: newspapers.com, ancestry.com, a data base at Emory University, Pitts Theology Library, and newspapers for the Atlanta Constitution from 1920-1933 for articles to enhance this history.

We interviewed many residents in the three-county area around Draketown—Haralson, Polk, and Paulding Counties. One older gentleman described walking to his first-grade class in 1939 in Draketown and noticing the broken photograph of a lady on the side of the monument. He ask several adults why the monument was there. "Oh, that's just something we don't talk about—something that's just better left alone." Quite a few folks we interviewed still did not know the story or were still not willing to talk about it.

We persisted. Many of these "third-generation residents" shared amazing stories of the older times. We recorded these old timers' stories and memories and used many to enhance and enrich the facts. These stories are probable, likely, and common of a culture of a small southern town in the 1920s.

We want to acknowledge those who took their time to help us by remembering what their family had always told them. These third-generation folks from Draketown and the surrounding area often put us on the right track to uncover documents and proof of what really happened.

We want like to thank: Richard Argo (editor), Judge James Baker, Hazel Barnes, Patsy Bollen, Barry Boyd, Betty Butler, Dorothy Butler, Novaleen Butler, Mike Campbell, Johnny Cantrell, James and Betty Ann Carden, Martha Goldin Church, Gene Cohran, Julie Butler Colombini, Cecil Dewberry, Deloris Durden, Maggie Edwards, Jana Gentry, Elaine Wood Gregory, Donald and Diane Hamil, Ruth

Holder, Judy Reeves Hoffman, Kenny and Susan Johnson, Ron and Nancy Lamar, Reverend Terrell McBrayer, Harold McCay of the Chattahoochee Methodist Church in Helen, Georgia, Gigi McKinlay, Joe Mosley, Robert Nix, Marcia Otwell, Richard Plunkett, Kathy Rechsteiner, John Reeves, Jr. and his wife, Anita Reeves, Reverend Wendell Rush, Harold T. "Todd" Slate, Daniel Swofford, Tom Upchurch, Lowell White, and Dr. Allen Wilburn. A special thanks goes to Steve Mullinax and John Bailey who accompanied us on many of our research trips.

The old adage, "we are richer for the experience" certainly applies here. Our greatest breakthrough came when we located Stewart family members in North Georgia who had kept photos, documents, and artifacts. Their oral and written history greatly enriched our search for the truth.

To understand history and to share the good and the bad times has remained our goal. We decided early to change some names to protect the families of those who were arrested and released or acquitted. We strongly suspected throughout this research that there was a conspiracy. The absence of records makes it hard to prove, but the very absence of so many records contributes to this suspicion. We uncovered crimes that were never brought to justice and people "who never paid for what they did." We sought to give the benefit of the doubt to the majority who did what they had to do to survive in hard times.

Draketown, Haralson County, Georgia

The small community of Draketown lies near the headwaters of the Tallapoosa River in Haralson County in northwest Georgia. Back in time, long before the white men came to this area, the Native Americans called these rolling red hills and fertile valleys, "Long Leaf."

In the mid-1800s, copper miners migrated south from Ducktown, Tennessee to Draketown, Georgia. They named the new community Draketown—no stretch of the imagination as to why they picked that name.

This new settlement soon had a grocery store ran by Mr. Green Carroll and Crow's Hill School, which gave the children an opportunity for education. Jim Frank Smith's grandfather built a dormitory for the students of Crow's Hill School. The Draketown Baptist Church was established on October 11, 1879 on land donated by Dr. W. F Golden (Goldin). Early members were J. H. Hestley, W. T. Hestley and S. T. Simms.

Several doctors came to the area. The first Draketown doctor was Dr. R. B. Hutcheson who was married to Ellen Hogue. Eventually three other doctors became residents here: Dr. William Franklin Goldin, Dr. Benjamin Franklin Eaves, and Dr. William Love Hogue.

With a grocery store, a school, a dormitory, and doctors, this little town attracted many residents. Next came a blacksmith shop run by William Morris, a cotton gin and gristmill run by Cissero Bishop, and a hotel built by Mr. Will Abercombie.

In 1905, the first steam-powered vehicle chugged into Draketown. In 1910, the first automobile came to town—a T-Model Ford owned by Dr. W. F. Goldin. A year later, four Maxwell cars were purchased by residents. Most citizens could not afford cars and traveled by horse and buggy or wagon. Both horse-drawn buggies or wagons and cars came through town. It took an entire day to travel one way by mule and wagon to or from the county seat of Buchanan where a railroad and scheduled trains came through town.

Little Draketown attracted new interest when it was publicized that an academy would be established in the town. Dr. W. F. Goldin donated ten acres for a Baptist College campus. On March 10, 1909, The Georgia Baptist Board of Education met in Atlanta with Dr. John E. White of the Second Baptist Church of Atlanta as its newly elected president. This session voted to coordinate all Baptist institutions into a general system, promote the endowment of the schools already in the system, and stimulate the effort to establish Baptist high schools or academies in every section of Georgia. Draketown Academy of Haralson was enrolled in the system with Mercer University at its head. A dormitory was built for students and a hotel for teachers to board during the school sessions.

This Draketown hosted "Baptist Institute" lasted from 1909 until 1918, closing at the end of World War I. The building was sold to the county; its students transferred to other colleges. Graduates took teaching positions within Haralson County and many enjoyed long careers until retirement. The two-story Baptist Institute building served as a public school for decades.

Draketown's history is one of a quiet, small farming community in a serene location. The typical head-of-household living near Draketown in 1900—1920 was a farmer raising corn, sugar cane, potatoes, cotton, or cattle, or working in the Draketown copper mines.

Trouble came in the early 1920s when the first unsuspecting North Georgia farmer noticed his crops were ruined. This devastating pest, the boll weevil, spread quickly to wipe out most farmers. The ruined crops, coupled with summer droughts, crushed the economy of the Deep South. With no money from the yearly harvest, God-fearing men become trembling, incensed fathers who looked each night at their hungry children with no idea how to feed them. There was no money for food in a time before welfare checks, disability insurance, social security, food stamps, and public housing allotments.

This boll weevil became the enemy. With crops eaten away, summer droughts, and the crippled economy, the Southern states faced times as difficult as those following the War Between The States which had ended only fifty-eight years before.

Many struggling farmers were the sons and grandsons of the Confederate soldier who had not returned from the Civil War or one who returned maimed, sick, and in desolate health. Old timers declared, "The boll weevil did as much damage as Sherman's army!" Now a new fight was on the hands of the Southern farmer—one they did not know how to overcome.

This poverty and lack of hope changed behaviors, destroyed marriages, and kept sick women from calling a doctor when they lay dying on the birthing bed: No money to pay a doctor. Grown men cried in despair. They turned on each other; courthouse records show an increase in cases of men fighting. One record described two men in a fist-fight over the debt of fifty cents. Warrants filed by wives against their husband for drunkenness, being out of control, and wife-beating were on the rise. Frustration was followed by the era of prohibition, January 17, 1920—December 5, 1933.

Prohibition in Georgia: In 1907, whisky was voted out of Georgia. Prohibition for the entire United States became law on January 17, 1920. By December 5, 1933 when Prohibition, the Great Experiment, was finished, the Federal Prohibition Enforcement Bureau estimated that 800 million gallons of illegal booze was flowing out of illicit distilleries and gin mills across the country. More was smuggled across the borders, with millions of gallons converted from industrial alcohol. Ships brimming with tanks of whisky anchored just outside the three-mile limit up and down the east coast, bearing booze for pickup by rum runners.

People boiled up whisky on their tiny "alky cookers," and Southern moonshiners had dollar marks in their eyes for the first time. They ran their stills overtime to meet the big demand from "fruit jar trade" around their communities and for the big markets up north.

The Prohibition Enforcement Bureau faced a full-scale, nationwide war on moonshining. The general estimation in 1925 was that a half-million Americans were tied to moonshining or bootlegging in some form. Agents captured 172,537 stills during that year alone! Between 1921 and 1925, still seizures totaled 696,993. But for every still seized nine remained undiscovered. In 1925, almost half the 2,200 prisoners in the Federal Penitentiary in Atlanta were locked up on liquor charges.

Many farmers, whose crops had failed because of the boll-weevil, struggled with their conscience before making illegal liquor for the first time. A man could work from daylight to dark, hoeing corn to sell for seventy-five cents a bushel. He could cut stove wood all day for a dollar fifty a cord. The likker business meant this same farmer could make ten times the money for less work.

Hopelessness was stamped on the foreheads of all who knew poverty and who were now beginning to understand hunger.

Introduction:

November 1988

One Saturday, 76-years-old Arreda walked into the beauty shop for Trisha to do her hair.

Arreda sat adjacent to the booth, waiting for Trisha, her beautician, to finish the customer in front of the mirror. She sat quietly thinking about things that had happened long ago—when she was a girl living in Draketown.

"Good morning Arreda. How are you doing this cold day?"

"Oh, I'm fine, I guess." She was a short, stout lady, but still beautiful, alert, full of fun, life, and laughter. Her fluffy hair was silver and her eyes shown a clear, bright blue. She made her way to Trisha and handed her the cane she carried, "so that she would not fall," and took a seat.

"About this time of year, every year, the memories come flooding back. I'm so glad I'm here today—it's all heavy on my heart. I feel like if I don't talk about it I'll burst."

"I can't wait to hear your stories," said Trisha. "I know the first time you came in to have your hair styled, you told me you would tell me about when you were living in Draketown. I think you said you were a child then?"

Arreda's thoughts returned to Draketown, "Yes, I was eleven years old in 1923." Arreda sat in the shampoo chair and leaned back. As Trisha ran water through her hair, Arreda started with an overview of Draketown in 1923:

In her mind's eye, she saw the layout of the cluster of stores and the houses scattered throughout this small southern town.

"My family lived in the old hotel, where teachers for the early academy had boarded. Running between the hotel and the next house, which was the two story, white board parsonage, was Gin Road that went down to an old cotton gin and to the grist mill ran by Cissero Bishop."

"Going east, past the parsonage, was Reeves' General Mercantile Store where my family shopped often; beyond Reeves' Mercantile was the Reeves' house. Next was the two story building where Lib Stephens' store, Stephens and Brooks, was located downstairs; upstairs, The Masonic Society—the Freemasons, and the Woodmen of the World met. Across another small secondary road, in the corner of the curve of town, was Dr. Benjamin Franklin "Ben" Eaves' office and behind his office was his house. In front of his office, was Will Morris' blacksmith shop, the Bank, the Post Office and on the corner was Oss Carroll's Dry Goods Store."

"Arreda," Trisha said as she walked across the beauty shop, "Come here and sit and tell me more. I can imagine all that you're saying, just like I'm there." Arreda with the towel on her wet hair made her way and sat in front of the mirror for Trisha to began rolling her hair in curlers. Here she continued describing Draketown.

"Across the road from Oss Carroll's Dry Goods Store was a one-story Victorian home with a porch that caused the entire structure to look like it wrapped around the curve in the road. The Lib Stephens' family had lived there for couple of generations. Running north past Lib Stephens' house was Gin House Road. Down that road was Doctor Goldin's large barn and beyond this barn was the cotton gin. In the late summer and early fall when the cotton came in, wagons lined up loaded down with cotton filling this road all the way to the Cotton Gin. The other end of Gin House Road connected to a thoroughfare going east and west across the county."

"West from Lib Stephens' home was a livery stable, a wagon yard, Dr. Hogue's office then his house, and several smaller homes lining the dirt road known as The Draketown Main Road. The west end of this main road took a sharp right and headed north to join up with the main thoroughfare running east and west known in those days as the Buchanan-Dallas Road.

"I lived with my family in the old hotel. There were a lot of rooms, but my family seemed to spread out and fill them up. Downstairs was the parlor, the kitchen and two large bedrooms, one for my parents, Jackson and Melviney Bingham; my daddy's twin half-sisters, Alpha and Omega, shared the other bedroom and they had a sewing room where they took in sewing for the public. Upstairs was my bedroom and one for each of my two brothers, Boots and Bud Bingham."

Trisha interrupted and asked, "Arreda, why was one of your brothers named Boots?"

"Well, his real name is Roy, but one Christmas when he was about twelve, he got a new pair of high-top black brogans. He was so proud of them. He kept them polished. Every night he went up to his bedroom early to polish his boots. We started kidding him about having so much pride in his shoes. One morning, Mama said, 'Go tell your brother, Boots, to come to breakfast.' After that the name stuck. When these boots wore out, he earned enough money on his own to buy another pair."

Dr. W. F. Goldin's house

Trisha finished rolling Arreda's hair and put her under the dryer. About a half-hour later, when she got Arreda from the dryer, she continued her story even before she reached the chair in front the mirror.

"East from the corner store was Dr. Goldin's two story elaborate Victorian house with a steeple, ginger-bread trim and an ornate wrought-iron fence which was said to have come from England, before the turn of the century. To the right of this wonderful home was Dr. Goldin's unpainted, clap-board office looking just as it did in the late-1800's. Beyond the old house was the Baptist Church then a grove of oak trees where the town folks had picnics. Just a little further east was the two story impressive, brick academy—later used as a common school—public school after the college closed in 1918."

Dr. Goldin's office as it looked in the late 1800's

"I had a little beagle, Buster. He was my shadow. He walked to school with me every morning. Whether he stayed there all day, I don't know.

But he was always there to walk home with me. He stayed on the front or back porch when the weather was warm or in the side room off the back porch, where the well was located, when it was cold."

"In 1923, the year before it all happened—those tragic events, we had a new pastor and his family to move into the parsonage next door to my family. What happened was in the newspapers all over the country."

Chapter 1
New Itinerate Pastor

November 1923:

An old man, riding in an old wagon pulled by an ancient mule, made his way up Temple-Draketown Road to Draketown. The wagon wheels squeaked and the corn in the back jolted every time the wagon hit a bump, rolling side to side in a rhythm with the wagon wheels.

A little girl who skipped happily to school with her little dog following her stopped to watch the comical scene coming toward her. The man wore bib-overalls and a sweat-stained slouch hat. He looked as old as the mule. The mule's big ears flopped back and forth as his head moved up and down. The old man could be seen every time the old mule lowered his head. But when the mule raised his head, it looked as if the man's hat was sitting between the mule's ears.

The old farmer called out to the little girl watching him, "I hear we're going to have a new pastor."

The little girl called back to him. "They're moving into the parsonage today!" He tipped his hat to the young girl, flicked the reins, and was on his way. The girl skipped on to school, followed by her dog.

The famous Reverend Robert "Bob" Stewart, his wife Alice "Wildie" Adams Stewart, and their two daughters Tannie, sixteen, and Lorene, five, was at that same moment moving into the Draketown parsonage.

The family was delighted to be moving into the well-kept, furnished, two-story parsonage on the main street of town. This parsonage was much better than some of the places the family had been assigned to over the six year of their experiences with Reverend Stewart's itinerate service to the Methodist Church. Alice said this place was just perfect the first time she saw the house her family would call home for a while.

The parsonage offered four rooms downstairs. The daughters each had a bedroom upstairs. The four rooms downstairs meant a parlor they would call the front room for guests who, more than likely, would be members of their new congregation and those who came requesting help and prayer. There was a kitchen and bedroom for Robert and Alice and a study for the pastor. This study was large enough for the pastor's small desk, a table for his typewriter, and several bookshelves they brought for his book collection. Many were Methodist literature and books on sermons.

Alice and Robert married on December 6, 1906, and lived in White County in North Georgia. After becoming a circuit pastor in 1915, he moved his itinerate family six other times, spending one to two years in each location. Being an itinerate pastor usually meant being a traveling preacher. Certain Sundays he preached at an assigned church. On other Sundays, he might hold a brush arbor revival in a section of the countryside that was too far from his church for people to travel.

At first, he served as circuit, itinerate pastor in the northern part of Georgia where both he and Alice had been born and where each of their parents still lived. Reverend Stewart and his family had served in Dahlonega, Cleveland, Dahlonega again for a second term; then, not too far away from home, Dawsonville. But in 1920, Bob was assigned to Whitesburg in Carroll County; then, transferred to Floyd County and Armuchee. Now they were making their new home in Draketown. The pastor's focus was the District Line Methodist Church which met the first and third Sundays of each month.

Some Armuchee church members who owned trucks carried the Stewart family's belongings—mostly in boxes—and a few pieces of furniture to their new home. Before the day was out and before the trucks were unloaded, members of the new congregation appeared at the door, smiling, nodding and shaking their hands. Alice was especially thankful for the covered dishes they brought.

Alice was accustomed to life on a pastor's salary. It was set yearly, according to the size of the family. That was it. Salary was not according to the size of the congregation, how many churches a pastor served, or the trips he made out to minister to the congregation on freezing cold nights.

Late that afternoon there was a knock on the door. Jesse Hogue from across the street came to welcome them to their new home with a jar of honey from her husband's hives. Jesse's husband was Dr. William Hogue. "Our house is directly across the street from you and my husband's office is in our side yard. Come visit anytime. I'm always home, but William is usually gone to visit the sick all hours of the day and at night sometimes." Alice immediately liked Jesse Hogue and promised to visit her.

The next day, the nearest neighbors, Jackson and Melviney Bingham, came bearing food and well wishes. Jackson Bingham greeted the pastor and helped bring in the fire wood for the wood-burning stove in the front room and the cooking stove in the kitchen. Melviney offered to help unload the boxes of books. Arreda, who was Jackson and Melviney's daughter, told Tannie she would meet her on Monday to walk with her to the common school to enroll. Arreda was younger than Tannie, but they got along fine; Arreda hit it off right away with the little girl, Lorene.

Draketown Baptist Institute, later the Common School, Courtesy Robert Nix.

On Monday morning, Tannie was waiting for Arreda. As they walked to school, Arreda told her about each building and acquainted her with the small town as they strolled south passed the Lib Stephens' house on the curve of the road. Next was old Dr. Goldin's glorious house with the steeple and the ornate, wrought-iron spindle fence. Arreda took a stick and dragged it along the fence where it bounced off each spindle to make a clicking sound. She pointed out the old rustic house that was the first Dr. Goldin's office, before the turn of the century. They continued south past the Baptist Church to a large open space and a grove of trees; on the right across from the church property was the cemetery. A little further down on the left loomed the brick two-story former Draketown Baptist Institute which was now the common school.

Arreda walked with Tannie to the office where she introduced her and left her to go to her classroom.

Over the next week, Arreda visited the Stewart household often. After they

1922 Draketown School, Courtesy Robert Nix

had each done their homework, played with Lorene's kitten, Snowball, and had a lively conversation, they discussed birthdays.

Lorene was first. "I'm five now; my birthday was on September 25th. I'm named Martha Loraine Stewart, but my nickname is Lorene."

"Well, I had my birthday in June; I'm eleven now. I have two middle names, Margaret Magnolia. If my daddy ever calls out 'Arreda Margaret Magnolia Bingham!' that means I've done something wrong and he is about to scold me," Arreda told her new friend and they both giggled.

Tannie looked up from a magazine and joined the conversation. "I just turned sixteen last week—before we moved. I had my birthday with my friends at my old church. My friends gave me a banjo."

She seemed a little perplexed at the two younger girls, but took this chance to let them know she was sixteen now and not happy with this last move.

Arreda gave Tannie and Lorene a questioning look when Tannie said she received a banjo for her sixteenth birthday.

"Oh, she plays lots of instruments. She plays the piano at church; she can play the guitar, and fiddle and the banjo. Mama says Tannie plays by ear. That means she can play any musical instrument and play any tune after she hears it just once," Lorene informed Arreda.

With that last remark, Tannie rose, went to her bedroom, and began playing her banjo, making up a lively tune and words as she went—reminiscing about "I've got friends far away, I miss them every day. Ummm."

Alice came to tell her it was late and she had better get home before dark. They each gave Arreda a hug and she was out the door; the night was cold and she ran quickly home. Buster, her dog, who had waited on the porch of the parsonage, was there to run along side her toward home.

The first Saturday in their new location in Draketown, Alice had finished unpacking the kitchen ware, put away all the clothes and was unpacking boxes of old newspapers and the rest of the books. The pastor was busy reading.

"Bob. Do you want these old newspapers from 1920?"

When he looked through what she handed him, he became animated and excited. "Oh, never throw those out! This was the beginning of Prohibition." He read and commented, "Billy Sunday. He is a most famous evangelist who was in great part, instrumental in getting the eighteenth amendment passed. The Volstead Act. You remember when all this happened. January 17, 1920."

"That's when we were in Whitesburg," she replied. "Just made the move from the mountains. Tannie was thirteen and Lorene was one and a half. I was busy as usual with the children, but I remember how all the protestant churches across the country rang the church bells at 12:01 a.m. The bell ringing at our church woke Lorene. She cried at first, but started to listen and smile. Then when the ringing stopped, she looked like she would cry. I rocked her back to sleep."

The preacher looked up, smiled at her comments about Lorene, and continued reading, "All across America there were 1,500 law enforcement officers just setting ready, listening to the bells ringing and glancing at their pocket watches. About 12:03, they went into saloons and restaurants that served alcohol, and started arresting. It didn't take long for the word to get around."

The pastor continued to search through the old newspapers. "Look here. Headlines, Funeral for John Barleycorn. A twenty-foot casket signifying the death of Demon Rum was put to rest. Twenty pallbearers escorted a horse drawn procession carrying the casket. America from coast to coast was urged to join the water wagon, forever."

"Billy Sunday's sermon, 'The reign of tears is over. The slums will soon be only a memory. We will turn our prisons into factories and our jails into storehouses and corncribs. Men will walk upright now, women will smile and children will laugh. Hell will be forever for rent.'"

"Here's another article about Billy Sunday. 'The liquor interests hate Billy Sunday as they hate no man.' Sunday replies, 'I will fight them till hell freezes over, then I'll buy a pair of skates and fight 'em on the ice.'" The pastor chuckles at this, folds the newspaper, lays it aside, and reaches for another one in the stack.

"I've saved articles from the W. C. T. U.—Woman's Christian Temperance Union of Georgia and the Georgia Department of Anti-Saloon League. Here is one where the Ku Klux Klan pledges to support the movement of Methodists Ministers in their fight against liquor use, making and transporting. The Klanmen vowed to support this Prohibition movement—The Great Experiment."

John Barleycorn serving Uncle Sam

Reverend Stewart folded all the papers and put them into a box to store on the lowest bookcase in the corner. "It's been over four years since the start of prohibition. We've still got a fight on our hands. When liquor became taxed and those making it refused to pay the tax, it became prevalent to make it in secret. It's a profitable business. But it kills. It's the root of most of the evil I see. I see a family starving because the man of the house is out drunk. Or another family man doesn't come home because he's in the Atlanta Penitentiary. Half the 2,000 prisoners there now were put there because of some illegal activity of moonshining or bootlegging. I plan on keeping up this war on evil that's hurting families across the nation and here in our own community." He finished putting away the newspapers, some sermons, and documents pertaining to the Methodist Conference.

On Sunday, Reverend Robert Stewart met his congregation at the County Line Methodist Church, a wide low white-boarded framed structure with a tin roof. The church had been established before the turn of the century. Many members of congregation were descendents of some of the first members. There were older members who were charter members. He, his wife Alice, and their daughters were well received. He delivered a memorable sermon attacking the "evil that creeps up on you."

"You go about your life as a hard-working, faithful member of the church, but there is evil all around you. It comes in disguises. You have to be on guard against slipping and back-sliding. Your neighbor may not be as faithful as you have been. Don't ever stray from God. Pray and read the Bible daily and He will sustain you in no matter what your temptations may be."

Reverend Stewart came out of his study late one winter evening after working on his Sunday sermon for hours and joked with the girls and Arreda who had just gotten up to get her coat and head home, "Oh, you're leaving? I thought I had three daughters," he joked, making the three of them laugh.

The phone rang. It was Dr. B. F. Eaves, the local Draketown doctor. He told the pastor, "You're needed at the Blivins' house. Right now. It's Chester; he drank lye. Go east, past the old College. About a mile. I'll park facing the road and leave my lights on."

Robert hung up and glanced at Alice who had just come from the kitchen when the phone rang.

As he was reaching for his coat on the hall-tree beside the front door, he told her, "I've got to go. It's the Blivins family. It's Chester; he's bad."

"I'm coming, too. They've got several children; maybe I can help," Alice grabbed her coat and looked at the three girls, "Arreda, can Tannie and Lorene go home with you?"

They each nodded, grabbed coats, and were out the door. Alice and Robert climbed into his older 1920 automobile and pulled out; Alice looked back to see the three girls head down the street to the Binghams', followed by Arreda's little dog.

In just minutes, they were at the Blivins' white frame farmhouse about a mile out of town; they had no trouble seeing Dr. Eaves' car with the headlights still shining toward the road. The two of them ran toward the house. Robert went to the car and turned the lights off after Alice made her way to the porch. In the house they saw a cluster of children and Marie Blivins around her husband lying on the sofa. Dr. Eaves was beside Chester trying to clear his throat; Chester Blivins was gulping and chocking, struggling to get air.

Austin, the oldest Blivins boy, about thirteen, met them at the door, crying. "He drank lye; he came in drunk and must'a fell asleep on the sofa; he must'a woke up and reached down for his bottle; I guess it fell over, under the sofa; he searched and grabbed the nearest thing. Mama had just cleaned the floor with lye—lye mixed with water, and tiptoed out of the room, for the floor to dry; she went in the kitchen and we had supper. We didn't even know he had come home, 'til we heard him hit the floor. Austin cried some more. "It's bad. I know it is. Mama said to get Doc Eaves. I ran all the way to his office as fast as I could."

Alice sat down with Austin in side chairs close by, gave him a handkerchief from her pocket and patted his shoulder, trying to console him.

The doctor straightened up and announced, "I want all of you including Marie to go into the kitchen with our pastor's wife, here," he nodded toward Alice, "I need to work on Chester."

As all the children and Marie went into the kitchen, Alice followed but looked back to see Dr. Eaves reach into his black bag.

Eaves grabbed a syringe similar to those used to clear a new-born infant's throat. After several attempts to clear the lye from Chester's throat, he had given the man some relief. But he had withdrawn only a small amount of liquid from his esophagus. Dr. Eaves sent Reverend Stewart to the kitchen for a glass of milk. He tried to get Chester to drink a little milk to dilute and wash the poison through his system.

After several minutes, he realized Chester was unable to swallow and pouring small amounts of milk into his mouth only choked him more.

Eaves, glanced at Stewart and shook his head when he saw the questioning look in Stewart's eyes. Eaves stepped back to relax for a second and glanced toward Stewart again, nodding toward their patient.

Reverend Robert understood and stepped forward, knelt and said a prayer to the Almighty to send peace to this man in his misery.

"Father, forgive his sins; send Angels to bear him up to Your heavenly place."

He leaned closer to Chester Blivins and asked, "Can you hear me?" Chester nodded ever so slightly.

"Do you believe in Christ and accept him as your Personal Savior—your Heavenly Father?" There was a slight movement of Chester's head in a nod signifying, yes. Robert finished his prayer and rose in relief.

Eaves drew the pastor aside to explain. "You see," Dr. Eaves said quietly with his back to Chester, "I was only able to remove a little liquid. Lye is thin like water. It went right down to the stomach after he swallowed the contents from the bottle."

They looked and there the half empty bottle still lay on the floor close to the sofa where Chester had dropped it. Not much was left to spilled out.

"The poison of it had already been digested into his system. He won't die of suffocation, but of poison. Let's get the family in here."

Reverend Robert went to the kitchen; the anxious eyes of Marie and their children looked to him. As they filed out of the kitchen to go back to the front room to see their daddy, Robert made eye contact with Alice, who had hung back to let the others go first, and shook his head ever so slightly making sure none of the children saw him communicate this to his wife.

Alice, Reverend Robert, and Dr. Eaves stayed the rest of the night. Alice put the two youngest children to bed. She rocked the baby to sleep, put her in the baby bed, and turned her attention to the five-year-old daughter.

As she put her to bed, the girl was tearful and asked, "Do you think my daddy will die?"

Alice replied, "Honey, the doctor is doing the best he can to help your Daddy. We'll just have to pray." Alice said a simple, little prayer and it seemed to soothe the child. Alice asked, "What is your name?"

"Oh, I'm Augusta Georgia because that's where I was born—in that town. Daddy used to travel; he'd work at a job, and when one played out, he looked for another job. My brothers, Austin and Dallas—they were born in Texas. Every time Mama had a baby, she named the baby for the town they were in at the time. I was born when we got back home to Georgia. So that's my middle name. Be sure and always call me Augusta Georgia. My baby sister, over there, that you just put in the baby bed, is Savannah. She was born in Savannah."

"You're a talker aren't you," Alice said as she pulled the covers around the little girl. I love all your brother and sister's names. It's time to go to sleep, now."

Alice had to smile at the humor in the middle of this grave situation. She turned out the lamp and at the door, paused, turned toward the little girl. "Good night, Augusta Georgia."

About 4:00 a.m., Chester passed. Alice sat with the two older boys, Austin and Dallas, trying to console them. In the early hours of the morning, the Stewarts followed Eaves back to Draketown. When they got back to the parsonage, they left their daughters with the Binghams since it would be daylight in a couple of hours. When they were inside, Robert sat down wearily on the overstuffed sofa and talked about the evening's events.

"That was one of the most heart-breaking situations I have ever seen. What a waste. A man lost his life and those children will have to grow up without a father and a wife will have to try and survive raising how many children?" He looked at Alice who sat in a smaller rocker with a devastated expression on her face.

"Four," she answered.

"Let us pray." Robert prayed for the Blivins family and for Dr. Eaves; then, he prayed for himself as a pastor to have the strength to face each day. Alice was in shock and weary. She did not want to hear another prayer. She wanted to go to bed. She closed her eyes tighter. She realized as a pastor's wife, serving the congregation and the community for that matter, she never knew from one day to the next, what each day would bring. As she fell asleep that night, she whispered a prayer for strength and patience.

As an itinerate pastor, Reverend Robert Stewart served several churches and held brush arbor revivals.

District Line Methodist Church, Courtesy R. Allen Wilburn

He was the pastor of District Line Methodist Church on the first and third Sundays of each month. On the second and fourth Sundays, he visited other churches in the area. He led revivals at several locations between "laying by and gathering" time for crops: early spring before planting, mid-summer, and in the fall after the harvest. An itinerate pastor holding a revival went prepared to stay with members of the congregation for a week.

The country miles stretching between established churches usually had a brush arbor about midway. These crude structures, made of six-foot oak tree trunks or beams, had open sides. The roof began with hog wire stretch across the top, with bushes and small tree limbs added for shade and protection from the elements. Clean-swept dirt floors were covered in sawdust and crude split oak logs formed long benches for the men on one side of the arbor. Ladies brought folding chairs and sat on the opposite side from the men, some watching their small children and some nursing their infants.

The country people traveled to these locations with eagerness and enthusiasm. Not only were these revivals for the renewal of their inner spiritual being, but for a boost of their social life which was nonexistent except for their immediate family. In the country where you had to walk for miles to see your closest neighbor, many times your family was your only contact for weeks.

Word went out over the countryside for months in advance and flyers were nailed to trees along the main roads.

FALL METHODIST REVIVAL
MOUNTAIN VIEW ARBOR
SEPTEMBER 21-25, 1923, 1:00 EACH DAY
REV. ROBERT STEWART, PREACHING

On the first day of the revival, horse-drawn wagons, vehicles, and pedestrians made their way, about noon, down dusty roads to congregate, greet their neighbors, catch up on the latest news, and sing praises accompanied by a fiddle or guitar. *Amazing Grace* and *Shall We Gather At the River* rang out across the 40-50 people gathered under the arbor. Tears of happy emotion moved several of the ladies.

Reverend Robert Stewart walked to the front of the arbor, placed his Bible on the crude log podium, and looked around at the congregation. He hit the Bible loudly with his fist and proclaimed, "We're here to take the hide off the devil!"

These beginning words straightened every one in their seat and brought children to attention. Then all heard a message, "Repent of your vices, throw your liquor, your tobacco, and your snuff out the window. Repent of your sinful thoughts and deeds, change your daily life and live more like your Lord and Savior, Jesus Christ. I'm here to ask the Father, the Son, and the Holy Ghost to renew your spirit. Do you feel deep down inside that your conscience is calling to you? That is the Lord tugging at your heart."

An hour later—at the end of the first day's service after the alter call but before the adjourning prayer, the pastor announced, "As you leave today, I will give a fan to each brother and sister. These were given to me by a funeral home to give out to the faithful. On one side is a depiction of the face of Jesus; on the other side is a denouncement of moonshining. Look at the face of Jesus and let that bring you back tomorrow. Also, bring your fan. It will be a hot tomorrow." A murmur of laughter rippled through the small congregation.

Courtesy Richard Argo

On each consecutive revival service that week, at least half of the congregation—the most faithful—sat listening to the gospel while fanning, creating their own personal autumn breeze.

A good revival usually brought ten to twenty souls to rededicate their lives to Christ and twenty souls to be saved. Reverend Stewart baptized by immersing or by sprinkling, whatever the new Christian wanted. A baptism for the new converts came at end of the revival. If immersion was desired, all went down to the creek, waded to the deep water, and held an old-fashion baptism.

"The creek water might be muddy, but the soul is washed anew—white as snow in the Lord," Reverend Stewart proclaimed each time he baptized. Though he was a small man, he could put the biggest convert under and bring him or her back to the surface in one graceful motion.

After the week-long fall revival at the Mountain View Arbor, Reverend Stewart came in the door chuckling and told Alice as she greeted him, "I've got something for my memoirs, if I ever write them. I heard an old-timer say, 'a revival is like a bath, it's only temporary, but it does you good.'"

Congregation Tears Down a Still

Reverend Stewart was instrumental in destroying a still in Floyd County, a county located north of Haralson County. He journeyed there one Friday to work with the local pastor. The entire church congregation had watched a still for weeks, trying to find it in operation. But while their members hid in the woods, watching, they could not catch the local moonshiners in the act.

Church members suspected activity on Sunday morning at the exact time of their Sunday service. So a few men from the church went early on Sunday morning to the site, hid in the woods, and waited.

Soon their patience paid off; several moonshiners silently slipped in from among the trees to set up the operation. When there was a roaring fire under the big, black metal kettle, when the moonshiners were stirring the mash, and after the drip of liquor appeared in the containers, these church people left. They hurried back in speeding automobiles to the sanctuary.

When they reached the churchyard, they parked, leaving the engines running, and ran into church as the congregation sang and interrupted, shouting, "The still is active! The still is active!" Most of the congregation dropped their hymnals and loaded up to follow the lead car back to the still. Some women and small children stayed at the church.

They were on a crusade. They barrelled in as far as the automobiles would go and ran up a steep path to the still to surprise the moonshiners. The screaming and hollering congregation was enough to drive the whisky makers into the woods to "run for their lives." Each church member brought an ax, staff, or long wooden board to destroy the still. One man produced a stick of dynamite. A big boom rattled the countryside for an instant. Limbs were blown off trees, a hole was blown into the side of the hill, and to this day, there in the woods in Floyd County lies the small pieces of that black metal pot.

Temptation is the devil looking through the keyhold.
Yielding is opening the door and inviting him in.
Billy Sunday

Chapter 2
Bad Times

November 1988

Arreda finished her story. "We all heard about the tragedy of what happened to Chester Blivins. His death and how he died was talked about all over the county. Then when the congregation up in Floyd County blew up a liquor still, that made the newspaper."

While Arreda finished telling about the congregation blowing up the moonshiner's still, Trisha finished the final touches to her new hairdo, then suggested, "Why don't we go have lunch at the cafe next door? I'm so intrigued with what happened back when you were young. I want to hear more."

At the cafe, they each ordered a sandwich and coffee. Arreda continued her narration, "Oh, times were bad back then, I remember . . ."

Purple-Hull Peas

Arreda was standing outside Reeves' General Mercantile Store when Owen Bollen returned from the market in Birmingham. He had gone there to sell the acre of peas he grew that year instead of cotton. The summer of 1923 had been a rough dry season. That day at the market, few people could afford to buy a half-bushel. A small, shy black woman approached him, looking at the peas.

"Sir, can I shell those peas for you? I would shell them for free, if you give me the hulls," she asked in a weak voice not much louder than a whisper.

Owen Bollen nodded and said gently, "That will be fine."

He would not charge extra for the peas she would shell; it wasn't costing him anything for her to shell. She had to be close to starving to ask for such. She would probably boil the hulls to make soup for her family, maybe adding some hog fat and serving it with cornpone—this would last a small family a few days.

Six Children Drink a Glass of Beer for Breakfast:

When school started, in early September, Arreda missed the Howard children. She saw one of the older boys on the road and asked him why they had not returned to school.

"I dropped out to help farm. But there's no crop. We're not going to school. We don't have decent clothes to wear—we only have what we wore all last year and this past summer. Daddy says there's no money for clothes. We go barefoot all summer to save our shoes. When we outgrow them, we pass them down to a younger brother or sister. We save our shoes for when it gets cold."

Late November was hog-killing time. The first frost of winter meant it was cold enough to kill hogs. Farmers cooperated, each helping the other. It was a big job. First the hog was shot in the head so the bullet went between its eyes and into the brain, killing it instantly; then, the animal was roped. The end of the rope was tied to a horse that dragged it to a chain mounted to a high strong limb or board-brace prepared by the farmer. The rope or chain was attached to the hog's hind feet to hoisted it high enough to work on so the front legs did not touch the ground.

Every farm had a hog-killing area. The gutting of the belly and the cutting-up of the meat would begin. Iron pots were set over a roaring fire to boil water. The boiling water was used to remove the hair from the skin of the hog until the scraping-to-remove-hair job was finished. It usually took all day; several men cut and brought in the meat to women in the kitchen who prepared and preserved it. Helpers were paid in meat. That was understood. It had always been that way.

Cliff Cole who lived on Villa Rica Road was ready to kill his hogs. He needed help. His father, Joe Cole, wasn't much help anymore. Too old. So Cliff went to Draketown to see Toby Howard. He knew of Howard and of his circumstance and he also knew Howard was a good worker. He knew this man had six children to feed and would probably be glad to get the meat in exchange for a day's hard work.

Cole knocked on the back door of Toby Howard's unpainted, weathered shack. He was let in by Howard's wife, Mollie.

"My husband will be back soon. Have a seat."

Cole sat by the fireplace on a stool and waited, observing his surroundings and thinking. There was a plain board table in the center of the tiny kitchen. It had a homemade oak bench on each side and a chair at each end of the table. On the table were six large glasses—one at each "place." There were no plates, utensils—forks or spoons—just the glass at each place.

As Cole waited, children drifted in, sat down, and waited at the table for their breakfast. These kids ranged in ages from three to thirteen. Cole thought to himself—one about every two years. That was typical. All were in stages of waking up and of getting dressed. A few of the older ones had changed the younger ones' diapers, maybe made a half-attempt at getting dressed themselves and in combing his or her hair. The younger ones were still in their nightgowns.

Cole got the impression that they had hurried to the table out of curiosity—to see him. They probably didn't have that many visitors, especially in their kitchen on such a cold morning. One little tow-headed girl, who had the brightest blue eyes, gave him a big smile. He returned the smile. The others looked at him with big, serious eyes—almost suspicious looks.

Early that morning, way before Cole had arrived at Toby Howard's shack, Toby left before sun-up, headed over the hill and into the woods and walked about a mile to where his Uncle James Hendrix and his two cousins, Owen and Hubert had set up a liquor still.

They hung a lantern high on a granite rock to shine over their operation. Each man had a schedule and duty. In a large barrel, they added water to ground corn, yeast and sugar or molasses, to make a mash. When the mash fermented, usually in twenty-four hours, it was dumped into a boiler; then, a lid was placed and sealed, and a fire was built under the mixture in the boiler. The steam flowed through the thumper and into the coils that were submerged in water to condense the steam into a liquid that dripped into glass jars.

Toby learned that using birch or chestnut wood was a way to avoid so much smoke with the fire under the big kettle. But he wasn't ready to get involved in likker-making. He skimmed the liquid off the fermented mash and filled his bucket. Then he headed home.

While walking home watching the horizon for the sun to come up, Toby Howard did some heavy thinking about the past year and how he had come to this point in his life. For the past five years, Howard had been a tenant farmer on Mr. Phillip's farm, and was used to getting a pretty good yield off 40 acres of cotton. Sharecropping on the Phillips' farm meant Phillips got a half and Toby kept half of the yield. If

Toby picked two bales of cotton, Phillips got one and Toby sold the other at the gin at the end of the season. Of course, Toby and his family lived in the run-down shack, rent-free.

Now every year the yield was less and less because of the boll weevil eating the boll on the cotton stalks. Since he could not read, he listened to the men up at Reeves' Mercantile talk about the little black bug that was infesting and killing the cotton boll right off the stalks. He heard that a dust called Calcium Arsenate could kill these pests. But it cost 8 and a 1/2 cents a pound. He talked to Reeves and Reeves told him every acre needed 30 pounds of dust on the plants. This kept the weevil from boring in.

"The cost of the dust was $2.55 per acre and forty acres would have cost hundred-two dollars," Reeves said.

Reeves had told him he could get enough for twenty acres from him and pay him when he sold the cotton at the end of the year. Toby also had to charge the cotton seed and the fertilizer to the store. He had always kept the seed from the previous year's cotton, got it when he took his yield of cotton to the gin in Draketown. Last year, there was such a small amount of seeds that when the cotton was ginned and the seeds, separated, he just sold the seeds. They would crush the seeds and sell the oil from the crushed seeds. But last spring when he planted, Toby wished he had kept the last year's seeds so he had not had to charge that to the store.

In the spring, Toby and his two oldest boys prepared the soil and planted only twenty acres in cotton seeds. In about six weeks, the stalks were nearly a foot high and showing signs of a boll beginning to bud. He went back to Reeves, bought cotton poison for twenty acres, and told Reeves he was ready for the cotton poison to be delivered.

Reeves delivered the six-hundred pounds of Calcium Arsenate and showed Toby and the two sons how to dust the plants. Reeves brought the barrels on his truck and stored them in the barn. Reeves showed the two oldest boys, Sandy, thirteen, and Gene, eleven, how to apply the dust. Each got a big square cloth to make a bag, put the dust in the middle, put in a bunch of small nuts and bolts in the bag, tied the ends up in a string, and walked down each row shaking the bag. The dust drifted onto the plants.

When the spring wind blew, a yellow dust rose over the rows of cotton plants in every field. The pungent odor was a common smell to the passersby.

In the summer, there was another problem—very little rain. Even though the dusting stopped the weevils from boring into the cotton boll, the twenty acres did not yield hardly enough to pay for the ox-guano fertilizer, the cotton seeds, and the poison. A bale of cotton goes for $20, less than five cents a pound. 'You couldn't make nothing on growing cotton' Toby thought to himself as he continued to walk toward home. Toby still owed Reeves so much money that he dared not show his face in that store. Toby Howard was so ashamed to be owing.

Howard brought his thinking back to the present. He realized his six kids would be up and hungry.

In a short time, Howard came over the crest of the hill from the woods and saw a T-Model parked far below outside of his little shack. As he walked, he carried a one-and-a-half-gallon bucket of liquid. When he started down the hill, he saw the footprints he made earlier that morning in the frost, imprinted footprints walking toward him, and realized that he needed to be sure and not wear down a path or trail to the still—to walk a few feet to the left or right each trip.

He had been walking fast, but he hurried even more now that he had seen a car at his house. Who was this at his house? He hoped it wasn't the revenuers.

The faster he walked, the faster his thinking. He owed so much. He had no money. There was nothing to sell. If he hired himself out to work, a grown man working from sun-up to sun-down could earn only 25 cents a day. That is if you could find anyone that had any money to hire help.

They were at rock bottom. His children were too ashamed of their old clothes to go to school. They went hungry. Some days they were literally down to starving. They wore the thin frames and hollowed-out faces of starving children.

In the fall, he had managed to grow some cabbage and collards. They would eat turnips and cornpone for Thanksgiving this year. Maybe he could trap some rabbits or shoot a couple of squirrels. They lived on squirrels. If he were lucky enough, he might go hunting and kill a wild turkey for Thanksgiving.

His thinking-and-walking that morning had brought him to a decision. He decided that he had better let these cousins know that he wanted to join them in their set-up. He had fought against getting involved in whisky-making for a long time. It was all around him. He had "studied on it" and decided to join his uncle and cousins in the moonshining business.

He was almost to the house.

Toby came in the back door. He handed the bucket to Mollie and turned; he was relieved when he recognized Mr. Cole, a fella he knew, sitting in his kitchen by the fireplace. He nodded and spoke. Cole got up from the stool and shook hands with Toby as Mollie took the dipper from the sink and dipped from the bucket, serving each glass. From the amber liquid and the faint smell of alcohol, Cole realized these kids were having beer for breakfast. They were eager to drink the first sips. They all responded as they were both thirsty and hungry. After a few sips, about half way of the glass, they slowed down and began to look up and listen to their daddy and this visitor.

"Howard, we're killing hogs tomorrow at my place. We need an extra hand. You interested?" Toby began to nod as Cole talked. Tears welled up in his eyes.

"Yes sir. Yes sir," he answered even before Cole finished asking. "That means I will have meat to feed these children." He glanced at the six eager faces and at his wife, whose face showed her relief and delight.

"We're starting tomorrow at daylight. That meant Toby would have to begin even earlier, taking his mule and wagon as early as 5:00 a.m. to be at Cole's before daylight. The roadway was sandy and there might be enough moonlight to see the sand in the road. He thought he could keep in the road until daylight broke. His mule knew the way.

"I'll be there. Thank-ya. Thank-ya. You can depend on me," he said as he shook Cole's hand. He and his wife exchanged glances as he saw Mr. Cole to the door. As the door closed behind Mr. Cole, Toby embraced Mollie. The kids were smiling, the younger ones not really knowing why, but the mood in the house was happier than it had been in a long time. They began talking excitedly—there seemed, right then, to be a little hope.

"If I do a good job tomorrow, maybe I'll be asked for other days and by other farmers," Toby smiled for the first time in months.

Toby thought to himself, 'I'll hold off on joining my cousins in their moonshine business.'

January 1924

At the Bingham household, the wood pile was small—most of the wood had been burned in the four fireplaces and in the wood-burning stove in the kitchen. Boots and Bud worked for months last spring and early summer, cutting trees, sawing logs, and splitting wood to stack in the wood pile under the covered tin building out back.

The shelves in the pantry off the kitchen were almost empty of the canning jars full of vegetables canned late last summer. On the higher shelves, the crocks of dried beans rattled, almost empty, but bushels of sweet potatoes from last fall's harvest filled the floor.

Melviney made the announcement to her family. "For the month of January we are eating in the parlor and keeping only one fire going—in that fireplace. By February the ground will be thawed enough to start a winter garden."

Late that next evening sweet potatoes were placed in the embers around the blaze in the parlor fireplace. Alpha built a fire in the stove in the kitchen and made cornbread.

For supper that night, the family ate at a small table placed in the center of the parlor. Each had a sweet potato and a slice of cornbread. The next night they had the same. On the third night, Arreda complained, "Cornbread and sweet potatoes again! I'm tired of that."

"Honey, if your daddy and Bud didn't work at the grist mill, we wouldn't have cornbread. When so many farmers came to have their corn ground up into cornmeal in the late summer, your daddy took his pay in the cornmeal. We stored the bushels in the pantry. That's why we have enough to last through the winter. There are months when farmers don't have any corn, so that's why in the winter Jackson and Bud are home—there's no work at the grist mill for them."

"Here, Alpha made butter today; that will go good on your cornbread," her mother said passing her a small dish of yellow creamy butter. Arreda put butter on her cornbread and on her hot sweet potato. Omega brought the sugar bowl from the kitchen, smiled at her and said, "Put a little sugar on your sweet potato, too." Arreda smile back, "Thanks."

March 1924

One cold spring day at school, all the students sat near the pot-bellied stove to keep warm while they ate their dinner—the noonday meal. Among the students were the Blivins children: Austin, Dallas, and Augusta Georgia. Tannie Stewart was a teacher's helper in preparing the lessons as she was one of the oldest and brightest pupils. Tannie always sat with Arreda's brother, Boots; Arreda was sure they were sweet on each other.

Arreda noticed several of her classmates had nothing to eat—not even a biscuit or a sweet-potato. Arreda shared what she had with the two Barber children—Johnny and Janice.

That night Arreda heard her Mom's crying. When she asked, "Mama, what's wrong?"

Melviney just shook her head and said, "It's about Naomi Barber. I don't want to talk about it now. I will tell you later." Her mother went to the bedroom and lay across the bed.

No Money to Pay the Doctor

Clyde Barber had been a man with not much to live for but work and more work on the farm. He was the youngest of a large family. Now that his brothers and sisters had all left home, it was up to him to make a living for his parents and himself—too big a job for such a young man. He had thought many times he wished he had never been born. He was just existing in a stale life.

More than eight years ago, when his dad, Oscar, fell off the porch and twisted his ankle, Clyde took him to Doctor Eaves in Draketown to see what he could do. His dad had been too drunk the night before to get into the house and fell off the porch trying to find the door.

When Clyde brought his dad into Eaves' office, he stopped and just stood there staring.

"What can we do for you sir?" asked the sweetest voice he had ever heard from the prettiest young girl he had ever seen.

He could not take his eyes off this slender, tiny young woman with long light, brown hair down her back. She was breathtaking. She stared at him shyly with big brown eyes. He just stood there, dumbstruck.

Dr. Eaves came into the room and asked, "Oscar, what have you done to yourself this time?"

He looked at Oscar who was leaning on a big stick he was using for a temporary crutch. Eaves took Oscar into his office, bandaged his ankle, and loaned him a crutch; then, told him to stay off his feet for a couple of weeks.

Out front, Clyde learned the pretty girl's name was Naomi Miller. He had a few minutes with her and got to know about her past. Her mother died when she was born and her sisters and a brother took care of her while her daddy farmed.

"They called me Baby until I was five years old," she told Clyde. "One day I announced, 'my name is Naomi.' I named myself and it took. I thought it was a beautiful name when I heard the preacher at church read it from the Bible. After my sisters and my one brother were all grown and left home, I was left to care for my dad. He died last winter."

After Naomi's dad died, she dropped out of high school at fifteen and came to Draketown to live with her aunt. She helped with the nieces and nephews and took the two-day-a-week job at Dr. Eaves' office. She did what she could to help her aunt and support herself.

When Clyde left the office with his dad that day, he could not get this pretty young woman off his mind. He smiled to himself when he thought about Naomi as a five-year-old, naming herself.

Clyde went to church Sunday at District Line Methodist Church, hoping Naomi would be there. He was in luck and saw her in the congregation; he sat as close to her as he could. After the last hymn, and the last prayer, he worked up enough nerve to nod and speak to her. When she smiled sweetly and said, "Hello," he thought his heart would burst.

Secretly Naomi was enamoured with this tall, slim young man with the big smile and tasseled blond hair and was thrilled to see him that day.

They were both at church the next meeting and sat together. Clyde learned what a hard time Naomi had as a child, "I went to school a few months in the first grade and when we moved I told the teacher at the next school I was in the third grade. She laughed her sparkling laugh, looking at Clyde with her big brown eyes. "I not only named myself, I promoted myself." They laughed together and he hugged her for the first time. Then he shared his story.

Clyde dropped out of school at sixteen to help his dad on the family farm. They had a small, white framed house and eighty acres planted half in corn and the other half in cotton. With the boll weevil and a relatively dry summer those last few years, he and his dad were discouraged after not making a living to support them and his mother, Telma.

The year-round gardens and the hogs they raised to kill, one each year, provided enough food for their family. They grew enough produce for what they needed and took the extra to market. From the money they made on produce, they bought staples like bacon, coffee, sugar, lard, and flour and every now and then, clothes.

The most unexpected thing happened—Oscar went missing. Early one morning, after Oscar's ankle was better, he was back at work plowing in the field and Clyde was in the house helping Telma can vegetables. They looked out several times over the morning and noticed Oscar out in the field, plowing the mule. Telma got the noon-day meal ready, set the plates and food on the table, and rang the dinner bell to call him in to eat, but he didn't come.

She looked out to see if he was on his way to the house. There was the mule and the plow just standing in the middle of the field, but he was nowhere around. Usually he brought the animal into the barn to cool off and get water while he had dinner.

At first Clyde searched the woods adjacent to the field. He saddled the horse and searched the other fields, thinking his Dad could have had a heart attack or heatstroke. He might be drunk or passed out somewhere. Clyde went back into the house where Telma awaited anxiously. She looked dismayed.

Clyde went to Reeves' Mercantile, Oss Carroll's Dry Goods Store, and to the Post Office. "Have you seen Oscar Barber?" He put his head in at the bank and looked around, then went to Lib Stephens'.

He asked everyone he met, "Have you seen Oscar Barber?" He stopped in at Dr. Eaves' office. No one around Draketown had seen Barber. He asked at the livery. One man, who had just come in with his mule and wagon, heard him.

"I saw Oscar this morning walking toward Buchanan, thumbing a ride. A car pulled over and he got in. The car sped off, going west on Buchanan Road toward Alabama."

He had just walked off and left the mule in the field, left his wife in the kitchen, and left Clyde to run all over the countryside searching for him.

The locals knew Oscar Barber was "bad to drink." It was obvious to everyone what had happened. He had just got fed up with trying to make a living for his wife and son who had dropped out of school to help. Everyone knew that Telma probably wasn't the easiest, nicest person to live with, either.

It wasn't an acceptable thing to do. It wasn't common, but it wasn't unheard of for a man to abandon his family, just leave and go to another state and "start over." This happened more often than divorce.

After a few weeks of looking, wondering, and waiting, both Telma and Clyde knew their husband and father had just "quit his family." Clyde was the man of the house and would have to carry on farming as best as he could. The first six months he did not do well. He had one less laborer, so he cut the planting to half—twenty acres of corn and twenty of cotton. He put his cotton seed and cotton poison on credit. He and his Mom continued to struggle. About this time he and Naomi began their courtship.

"Every time I look around, Clyde, you're here in the office," Dr. Eaves said with a smile. "What can I do for you today?"

"I just came by to say Hey to Naomi." He grinned and glanced at her. He thought about her all the time. He called her "Sunshine" because she had brought sunshine into his life. Clyde had something to live for now. He felt that Naomi saw something in him that he had not seen in himself, up to now. They married three months later and she went to live on the Barber farm with Clyde and his mother.

Clyde had been her 'knight in shining armor;' he had saved her from her loneliness. She had a void in her life from not having a mother. She craved a mother.

The first day when she met Telma, she looked forward to seeing her, thinking she could be that mother figure she never had. Right away she knew Telma was jealous of her, did not want her around, and thought her an interference. But Naomi did not let Telma and her ways bother her. She loved Clyde and loved being married.

When Clyde and Naomi's first child, Janice, was born, she had never been happier. She loved being a mother. She had become a mother to her Janice that she had never had.

Clyde and Naomi had been "getting by" the last eight years. They now had two children; Janice was now seven, and Johnny, six. Now one more was on the way.

After supper, the house was quiet; Janice was reading the school primer to little Johnny and Telma was sewing.

"Let's go for a walk," Clyde said. Naomi grabbed her sweater and slipped it on as they left the house. Holding hands, they walked to Frog Creek about a half mile from their farmhouse.

"I feel so big. I feel like I'm waddling!"

"Well you *are* nine-months pregnant," Clyde replied looking at her tenderly, squeezing her hand.

Clyde had built a little bench for them to sit on and watch the babbling creek.

As they watched the setting sun sink below the horizon, Clyde thought, 'I don't know how to make a living out of this barren dry land. The summer of '23, there was very little rain. Maybe this year will be better.'

He shivered and had a sinking feeling—one of a heartbreaking sense of loss. "I have this weird feeling like somebody just walked over my grave," he said to Naomi. She looked at him, concerned. He brushed his comment aside.

At that moment, he reached down, found a four-leaf clover, and to change the mood showed her the clover, "Look. I found a four-leaf clover."

She took the four-leaf clover and fingered each leaf as she repeated, *"One leaf for fame; One leaf for wealth; One leaf for knowledge; One leaf for health."*

Little did either of them know that in three days Naomi would be dead.

When Naomi's pain started, she had been struggling with the wash, boiling the clothes in a big wash pot outside. Telma had helped some, but these "weren't her kids' clothes to wash."

Clyde was working in the early spring garden where he had grown a few cabbage, turnips, greens, and onions. He saw from the garden when his wife fainted. He ran to her, picked her up, and carried her inside to bed. No sooner than she regained consciousness than the moaning began. Clyde knew it was time to go for Dr. Eaves. Before he could get to the front door, he ran right into his mother.

"Where do you think you're goin?" she growled.

"I've got to go for Doc Eaves. Naomi fainted and now she's in labor."

"And whose going to pay Doc Eaves? You still owe him from the last time she fainted. I can deliver that baby," she snarled. "You get back to work and I'll call you."

After an hour, Clyde Barber wanted to be away from the house. He could not stand her screaming. He sat out back of their little farmhouse, just far enough away so as not to hear the screams. He thought about all that had happened this year. No crops for the first time since he had married.

Those pests—the boll weevil had eaten the plants before they had time to bare the blessed-white cotton. Just as the boll first grew on the cotton stalk, the weevil boar in and laid an egg; then, the boll fell to the red clay ground and would not bare the cotton. The newly-hatched and the one that laid the egg both found another cotton stalk to bore into the first boll that appeared. The cotton never got a chance to produce.

Clyde had read in the newspaper how this destruction of the cotton crop came about: The boll weevil crossed the Mexican border in 1898, got to Texas about 1910, to Alabama about 1915 and was full-blown in Georgia now in 1924.

Farmers took several years to realize the devastation. Some just changed the crops they grew; some tried a crop of corn, syrup cane, or peas. Some tried tobacco for the first time, but you had to know what you were doing when it came to the harvest and drying of tobacco.

Others, who would not give up attempting to out-do the weevil, tried burning their fields. But that required cooperation. If the farmers on each side of his farm did not both burn, they could each inherit the weevils from the burned field which had escaped through the air or floated with the smoke.

Just to get the seed and fertilizer, Clyde had mortgaged his mule at the bank. For his 800 pound red mule, Big Red, who was about 14 years old, he got $185. At the end of the season, he was unable to pay the bank. He had to sell his mule, but no one had $185. He let the ole' man Jones have that mule for $85, and he still owed the bank $100.

Barber scrounged around, selling the eggs his chickens had laid. His wife made butter from the milk his one cow had given. The grocery store did not give full credit for the butter and eggs, because he owed so much for the food and supplies he had gotten during the previous year. They kept a percentage toward that payment on his debt. His wife dried and canned only a few vegetables from the small garden because she was not that strong. Never had been. And with the baby . . .

Clyde Barber looked up to see his Maw standing at the stoop at the back door; she was waving to him. He ran expecting to be shown a new son or daughter.

"Yor wife's in trouble. That baby of yor'n is not moving. That's what you git for havin' another kid. Y'all can't feed the ones you got now."

Clyde ran into the house, "Naomi!"

He did not know what to expect. There lay his wife, her face white as the sheet where she lay. He had not drawn a breath since his Maw had told him Naomi was in trouble.

"Naomi!" She moved her head slightly and barely opened her eyes. He saw the bundle wrapped in a stained towel lying on the table. The baby looked like a pale, lifeless doll. Just as he thought the baby might be dead, it moved ever so slightly.

He didn't care. He didn't care that he had no money. He ran. He ran to town—

to Dr. Eaves.

Clyde hit the door of the office hollering, "Doc, come quick. Naomi's bad-off. She had the baby. It's hardly moving."

Dr. Eaves grabbed his bag. Both jumped into his car. They were at Clyde Barber's farmhouse in minutes.

"You should have called on me. You know I would have come."

"I can't pay you."

"You could have paid me later."

In exchange for his services, Dr. Eaves, many times, was given a chicken, a bundle of turnips—once he was given a puppy as payment for his "doctoring." Folks said that Dr. Eaves had probably delivered every baby in Haralson County within his time of practice as a doctor there.

Eaves went into the farmhouse and to the back bedroom where he found Naomi weak and lifeless. She lasted an hour and slipped away. Dr. Eaves determined the baby had been breech after examining Naomi and asking Telma a few questions. With the strain of trying to bear the child, Naomi probably had a heart attack. He did save the baby boy, but he was underweight and his breath was shallow. He could have saved Naomi if Clyde had come for him when labor started. He could have turned the baby; it would have not been breach, and Naomi would have delivered safely. But he didn't say that to any of them. Telma stayed in kitchen, but she listened to the conversation between the doctor and her son.

He called on Telma to prepare the body—to wash and wrap it in a sheet. Dr. Eaves went back to his office where there was a telephone; he made arrangements for Naomi's burial. He wondered what would happen to the tiny baby.

By that afternoon, when their son and daughter, Johnny and Janice, came in from school, they gathered around to stare at the form wrapped in a sheet, on the bed; Johnny looked confused.

Janice was crying and said, "Why did this happen?"

Telma had the limp baby, but they were too upset about their mother to look at their new baby brother.

Back at his office in town, Dr. Eaves shook his head, "I keep seeing this. This poverty. What's going to save these people? This hurts. I was especially fond of Naomi. She was a good, caring mother and a wonderful wife to Clyde."

Draketown Tragedy

Reverend Stewart Ministers at the Barber Funeral

The day after Naomi Barber died, her funeral service was held at the District Line Methodist Church. Clyde Barber, with Johnny and Janice and Clyde's mother, Telma, stood by the coffin and greeted the people who came to pay their respects. Telma was holding a tiny bundle wrapped in a blanket—the new son, Clyde, Jr. Telma wore a thin cotton dress and a large sweater pulled close around her. Her hat had a low brim and kept her eyes on the floor; then, she glanced up as people came to shake their hands in condolence.

Several couples felt obligated to show an interest in the new baby. When they came near Telma to see the baby, each was surprised at his paleness and lifelessness. They nodded politely.

Telma informed these couples who peered at the baby, "He's asleep. Let him sleep." With saying that, she wrapped the blanket closer around the baby.

Telma told everyone she met as she glanced toward the coffin beside the family at the front of the church, "I did the best I could. But she died anyway. It's not my fault."

Many neighbors came. Dr. Hogue and his wife, Jesse, sat with Alice Stewart, Lorene, and Tannie. Jesse and Alice had visited each other several times a week over the last months. Both their husbands had important jobs in the community and were away from home a great deal, the doctor with his patients and the preacher ministering to members of his congregation. Jesse was a great support to Dr. Hogue as Alice was supportive of Reverend Stewart. Each of their wives found a camaraderie beneficial to both. Jesse knew who was sick and needed help. Alice knew who was in need, so they worked together in their own ministry to the community and over these last months had become very close. Today they

Agnes Pearl "Jesse" McBrayer Hogue
Courtesy Barry Boyd

were there to support the Barber family.

Dr. William Love Hogue
Courtesy Barry Boyd

At the funeral Arreda Bingham and her parents, Jackson and Melviney Bingham, sat just behind the Hogues and Alice and her daughters. Jackson Bingham's two spinsters sisters came also—Alpha and Omega. Dr. Eaves and Nettie sat with Pearl Reeves. Mr. Reeves could not leave the store to attend. Arreda saw Janice and Johnny Barber with their daddy and grandmother siting on the front row. She felt really sorry that their mother had died.

Reverend Robert Stewart preached the funeral. Arreda gave a start when the preacher hit the pulpit with his fist. She sat behind Tannie and Lorene studying each of them. Both had nice coats and Lorene had on a flapper hat. Arreda was envious. She had seen those hats in the newspaper and told her mother she wanted a flapper hat. They were well behaved and friendly to the congregation and smiled at everyone as they came into the church. Arreda noticed they acted different that day, kinda like "how-the-preacher's-daughters-were-susposed-to-act" behavior.

Arreda's attention returned to the pastor as he walked back and forth across the front of the church. He read from the Bible, and they all stood and sang a sad song, *Open the Pearly Gate*. As the small congregation sang, Arreda thought about the words. These were sad words, but maybe a comfort to the family:

Open the Pearly Gate
1) Sweetly the heavenly breezes we hear
Falling upon the departed saint's ear,
Angels of peace 'round her death-bed await,
And they will open the pearly gate.
2) Earth with its failings and fadings are past,

> Surely the life is approaching at last,
> Calling the soul from its earthly estate,
> Angels will open the pearly gate.
> 3) Trusting and leaning on Jesus our friend,
> Thro' the dark valley His aid He will lend,
> Carry the soul to its heav'nly estate,
> Jesus will open the pearly gate.
> 4) Whispering angels are flying around,
> Ready to carry the soul to its home
> Over the river sweet messengers wait,
> Let them now open the pearly gate.
> Chorus: Open the gate,
> (Bass: Open the beautiful pearly gate,)
> Yes, open the gate
> (Bass: Yes, open the beautiful pearly gate,)
> Over the Jordan the angels await,
> And they will open the pearly gate

After Reverend Stewart prayed to dismiss, the funeral was over and the small congregation rose to leave. The preacher went down the aisle first, next the coffin, then the family, and then the other church members and people from Draketown who came to pay their respects.

As Reverend Stewart walked down the aisle to the back of the church, his coat flopped open on the right side just as he passed Arreda. She was very surprised to see a pistol tucked in his belt. Confused, she thought to herself. 'I though just the sheriff carried a gun. I didn't know that a pastor would carry a gun.'

Interment was back at the Draketown Cemetery, several miles from the District Line Methodist Church. The congregation waited in their automobiles as the coffin was loaded onto a truck which led the funeral procession back to Draketown. As the cars parked, several families followed Reverend Stewart and the Barber family down the path to the cemetery.

It was a cold, brisk March day. Arreda looked up and studied the pear trees lining the path as they walked; she admired the beautiful white blossoms when a sudden gust of wind showered them with the white pedals falling from overhead.

A prayer was said and the coffin lowered. It was heart-breaking just to be there.

As everyone left the cemetery, Arreda heard Clyde Barber tell a neighbor, "How am I going to take care of my two kids, my new son, and my mother and not a drop of money or any way to make money?"

Arreda was beginning to understand the phrase, "Times are bad."

A few nights after Naomi's funeral, Clyde lay in bed with his son Clyde Junior on his chest. He pulled a handmade quilt, Naomi had made, up over them. The full moon, shining through the windows nearby, illuminated the room. He thought about his sweet wife being in the arms of Jesus just like he was holding his son on his chest. He had to trust that she was in a better place.

Fear:
Afraid to smile; afraid to frown
Afraid to look up; afraid to look down
Afraid to live; afraid to die
Afraid to laugh; afraid to cry
Afraid to stand up; afraid to fall
Afraid to get up and be counted at all
Afraid of the day; afraid of the night
Afraid of the dark; afraid of the light
Afraid of the wrong; afraid of the right
Afraid you'll get hurt if you get in a fight
Afraid to sing; afraid to pray
Afraid to be silent; afraid to say
Afraid to eat; afraid not to
Always thinking about what I should and could do.

Chapter 3
Why Stewart Hates Alcohol

November 1988

After Trisha and Arreda finished their sandwiches and coffee at the cafe, they lingered, Arreda telling, "When I heard Clyde say he had not a drop of money or any way to make money, it broke my heart."

Trisha said, "Well, I've got a customer coming for a perm, so I best be getting back to the beauty shop. Why don't I put you down for next Saturday for the last appointment before lunchtime? That way, when we're finished with your hair, we can come back to the cafe and have more time for you to reminisce. I'm enjoying this."

The next Saturday, Arreda came early and continued with the same day of Naomi's funeral.

In the afternoon after Naomi's funeral, Lorene came over to visit Arreda. They were as compatible as a five-year-old and a eleven-year-old could be in that they both had a sense of humor, were intelligent, observant children, and each liked to have fun. They sat on the porch each rocking in a rocker, one on each side of the front door.

It was Saturday afternoon and time for entertainment in watching those who passed by the house on the Draketown Main Road. Arreda's beagle, Buster, slept on the steps totally unimpressed with anything that was happening.

Passers-by were a great source of the afternoon entertainment: there was the old farmer who came to town for guano, seeds, and sardines. He rode in the same wagon, pulled by the same mule he owned for the last fifteen years—since 1909. Then came the ancient farmer, age seventy-five, walking to town wearing overalls and his grey Confederate kepi cap—the one he wore when he fought in the War Between the States when he was sixteen.

The Draketown Hotel where Draketown Baptist Institute teachers boarded from 1909-1918. From an old newspaper—Courtesy Martha Goldin Church.

Suddenly they heard a roar and a braking sound, which caused some excitement on the road when a new, shiny black 1924 Ford T-Model roadster came speeding by and scared the old soldier right off the road.

"There goes Dub," Arreda announced. Both girls squealed and laughed as they continued to rock.

When the roadster roared by, chickens scratching in the dirt at the road-side squawked and scattered. When the dust cleared, one lay dead in the dirt.

Arreda ran to tell her mother, "Dub just killed a chicken with his roadster!"

By the time they got back to the porch, someone had picked up the chicken—probably to carry it home and put it in a pot for dinner.

The rolling store, a bus loaded down with merchandise from Oss Carroll's Dry Goods Store, rumbled by on the way to the country to peddle goods. The driver, Captain "Cap'n" Boyd, drove carefully on the way to visit his customers. He knew every person in those parts and even knew what they needed before they did, it was said. Cap'n packed extra fabric—some floral and some checked as he knew Minnie Hawkins, down at Five Points Road, was planning to make dresses for her girls. He picked out the print they would probably like. He knew that all four of her daughters would have a new dress, just alike, to wear to church within a few weeks.

Everyone in these parts knew what day the rolling-store came by their place, sometimes watching all morning and running out to meet the bus when it stopped by each house to sell or barter for fresh vegetables or eggs in exchange for fabric, sugar, or coffee. The rolling store was a life-saver to those who could not always make the trip into town.

Many men waited for the rolling store. Some waited at the house, others plowed their land closest to the roadside. To the men, the rolling store offered tobacco, extra plows, a few tools, but his best selling item was stored in a crate under the low shelf of canned goods. There in the crate were a dozen pints of corn whisky sloshing in the fruit jars. His first stop after leaving Oss Carroll's Dry Goods was to pick up these pints from his "source." Every time he sold a pint, he pocketed the money and celebrated by taking a swig from his own jar hidden under the seat in a bag.

Toward the end of his route, one little girl told her mama, "I like Cap'n but he smells funny." The mama just nodded and bought what she needed, smiling at Cap'n, ignoring the smell and what her daughter had said.

Cap'n Boyd had good reason to drive the rolling store so slowly over the countryside. He didn't want to break the pints and he didn't want to run off the road. By the time he got back to the dry goods store, he was feeling good.

As Arreda and Lorene continued to rock and watch the happenings in Draketown that March afternoon, Tannie came over to see Arreda's aunts, Omega and Alpha. She needed their services as seamstresses to sew her a new dress. She brought them a pattern and fabric that she purchased at Oss Carroll's store. She told them exactly how she wanted her new dress made. The twins could take the sleeves from one pattern and the neckline from another pattern and create just what their customer wanted. They could even look at a dress in a magazine and make it.

After Tannie left, it was late afternoon and the girls had to give up their rocking chairs to Alpha and Omega. As they each settled down in the rocking chairs, Alpha explained, "I just can't get over this new style. The dresses are long waisted with a band around the hips and the skirts are so short—coming just below the largest part of the calf-of-the-leg. Tannie said that's what the fashion magazines show, so we have to make it like the fashion magazine." Alpha rolled her eyes.

"Well that's the new look," Omega replied as she settled her heavy body into one of the rockers. "I don't know what this world is coming to. First, women had to have the vote; then they cut off their hair short and wear those tight caps instead of hats. In Tannie's magazine, I saw an ad showing a woman smoking a cigarette. I've never seen anything like it. The other day, would you believe, I saw a woman driving a car!"

The two old ladies still dressed like the last generation, wearing long printed-cotton dresses. Each twisted her hair on the top of her head and wore a bonnet. On Sundays they each wore a long black dress and a big black hat, the same style they wore in their youth before the turn of the century.

That afternoon after Naomi Barber's funeral, the twins had finished their getting-ready-for-Sunday duties. They prepared Sunday dinner so it would be ready after church. It was considered a sin to cook on Sunday. They fixed enough to have plenty left for the evening meal. They laid out clothes for everyone in the family for the Sunday service.

They told Arreda to shine her patent leather shoes so she would be ready for church in the morning. She went into the kitchen, got a biscuit, and came out with her Sunday black, patent leather shoes. She sat on the steps and shined her shoes with the biscuit until all the crumbs had fallen off the steps onto the ground. Buster was there to lap up every crumb. When she finished, Arreda's shoes were so shiny she could almost see her reflection.

After she put the shoes back in her bedroom, Lorene and Arreda watched Alpha and Omega rock in the rocking chairs, dipping and spitting their snuff. Sometimes they would spit in cans, but today they spat off the edge of the porch.

Arreda whispered to Lorene, "Who do you think can spit farther?"

Lorene replied, "I think Alpha."

"I think Omega." They watched for a while, giggling when each spat, projecting off the porch. Just as the young girls were giggling at the twins spitting off the porch, Melviney called the girls in to run an errand. They never learned who could spit farther, Alpha or Omega.

"Go to Oss Carroll's and get salted fish and hoop cheese. You know the salted fish is in the big barrel that sits close to the middle of the store. The cheese is covered with a woven cover on the counter. Here you can have an extra nickle for two of those large oatmeal cookies—one for each of you.

After the two girls went into the store, they got what they were sent to buy but looked around a bit. Lorene observed, "I've never seen so many things; I could look all day and not see it all."

"Daddy says, Carroll's Dry Good Store has everything a person needs from the day he is born until the day he dies. Daddy says Carroll even has coffins ready in the store room if anyone dies," Arreda informed.

They looked for a moment toward the store room."We better get our oatmeal cookies and head home," Arreda said. "Mom will be wanting to start supper."

They walked home eating the cookies. Arreda waved to Lorene as she went across the yard to the parsonage. Tannie sat on the front porch playing a slow tune on her guitar. She was so absorbed, she never looked up. She also saw Jesse Hogue on the porch with Alice, both in a serious conversation about sickness in the community.

Arreda in a cotton field in Haralson Co.

"Alice, we've got to get some help for that family, with the mother in bed there's no one to watch after those small children." Alice told her she would get some church members to take turns helping out there.

When Arreda went into the kitchen she heard a lot of boiling in the pots on the wood-burning stove and the smell coming from them was really strong. For supper that night, Melviney prepared the salted fish, collard greens, white beans, and fresh-baked cornbread with fresh, churned butter. They all sat quietly, eating. Arreda noticed Alpha mixed her collard greens and white beans in the same bowl, adding lots of hot soup from both pots. She also noticed that Alpha crumbled the cornbread on top of the beans and greens.

As they were about finished, Alpha lifted her bowl and drank from it like she was sipping coffee from a cup. She said in between sips,"Um, I love this pot liquor." When Arreda heard the word *liquor*, she snapped to attention and said automatically, "You'll go to hell for that!"

Jackson and Melviney looked up at Arreda. Her daddy asked, "What did you say?" Omega giggled.

"Alpha said she is drinking liquor. I said, 'You'll go to hell for that.' That's what Reverend Stewart says, You'll go to hell for drinking liquor." Arreda replied looking very serious.

Bud, her brother, regarded her scornfully from across the table. Boots laughed so hard he fell backward out of his chair.

"Boots. Boots. It's not that funny. Son, get up off the floor and apologize," reprimanded Jackson.

Boots, getting up offered a faint, "Sorry," but started chuckling again.

Jackson had to grin. "Honey, this is different. The soup that's left in the pot or bowl when the vegetables are gone is called pot liquor. Arreda looked relieved, but gave a mean look at Boots. Alpha just finished her soup and ignored the entire conversation. Omega giggled again.

That night after Naomi Barber's funeral, Arreda heard her daddy reading the newspaper to her mother in the parlor. Alpha and Omega had gone to bed after they cleaned the kitchen and Arreda was asleep in her bedroom, they thought. But when she heard Reverend Stewart's name, she roused up to listen. Pastor Stewart was her pastor and she heard him preach every first and third Sunday. She wanted to know more about him and why he carried a gun. So Arreda slipped on her robe and went to sit on the top step of the stairway to listen.

"I see here where Reverend Stewart is being called "The Raiding Parson" because of his stand against liquor."

Jackson began reading from the newspaper, "'He preaches every Sunday against the making of, distributing of, and consumption of liquor of any kind. The other six days of the week, he's out tearing up liquor stills. He and a few of his most faithful churchgoers scour the countryside until they locate a still. Whether it is active, deserted, or in operation at the time, they go out and destroy. With an ax, they chop holes in the kettles, making sure these kettles cannot be used again. They usually throw a rope around any standing barrels and hook the other end of the rope to the back bumper of the preacher's 1920 Ford T-Model. They start the car and drag what there is until it is unusable and persist until it is unrecognizable.'"

"'Many stills, deep in the woods, can't be reached by automobile, so they go on foot equipped with whatever they may need in order to destroy, obliterate, and remove the operation and run off the operators.'"

"'Back in July a year and a half ago—in 1922, when Reverend Stewart was an itinerate pastor in Armuchee, in Floyd County, he had been threatened with death because of his activities against moonshiners. The moonshiners actually put a note of warning—tacked it to the front door of the parsonage.'"

"The note read: 'We have had enough of stills being destroyed in this settlement. We will give you one week to get away. If you don't, someone will have to take care of your wife and children.'"

Jackson shuffled uneasily in his over-stuffed chair and rubbed his head, telling his wife, "When those moonshiners put the note on his door he turned it over to the prohibition officers and announced his intentions to continue his crusade. He told everyone, and it was in the newspapers what he said, 'I know how to handle a gun, and will not hesitate to use one if occasion demands.'"

Jackson lay the newspaper aside and said, "I'm worried about Reverend Stewart—Bob."

She looked at him with concern. "Bob's been warned, to cease his activities, but he has refused. Before he came to this county, he was active in the prosecution of liquor law violators in Lumpkin County where he destroyed thirty-nine stills within three months."

"Since he came to Haralson County in the fall of 1923, there had been open warfare started on liquor-runners and moonshiners here in this county," commented Bingham. He picked up another newspaper and read to Melviney.

"Well, it says here, 'He is a man who practices what he preaches, so he participates in search and destroy missions for local moonshine stills. He had been responsible for countless arrests and has personally cleaned out more than a score of stills and arrested their operators."

Melviney Bingham said, "I know he has a pistol on the pulpit beside his Bible. I've seen it. I've also seen the cartridges in his belt and know when he leaves the pulpit, he puts the gun in a holster on his belt. I just don't know if that's right. A pastor with a gun. Seems to me, it ought to be the Sheriff's business, not a preacher's business to be out there destroying stills. It sounds dangerous to me. I worry about it for Alice, and I worry about it for his daughters."

"This article talks about his unleasing powerful sermons against the manufacture, sale and use of spirituous liquors. 'Reverend Stewart's been here almost six months, and the news of his efforts to close the lid on the alcoholic beverage business has spread like wildfire through the woods from Harralson to Paulding County.'"

"Well, Bob is getting a reputation for being a fearless leader. He told me he's trying to bring stricter enforcement of the prohibition laws. It says here, 'Thus began the sensational warfare on liquor-runners and rum-makers in the Haralson, Paulding, Polk section of northwest Georgia. Since he has been in charge of the church at Draketown he has participated in a large number of raids upon illicit distilleries and violators of the prohibition law, and his unqualified zeal in this direction incurred the displeasure of those engaged in the illegal liquor trade.'"

Jackson Bingham continued telling Melviney, "I talked to Reverend Stewart last week at his parsonage. He told me about the many raids he and members of his congregation have been on this last year. He calls it fighting against the evils of liquor."

"I've met his assistant and right-hand man, Guy Austin. They have a schedule and have members of the church signed up for certain days of the week to accompany him. They try to send out no less than five men together every day. They also go out all hours of the night and early morning trying to find active stills. Even the women join in with the men in being forever watchful around the community and countryside for hints when things seem like they are just not right. When they do locate an active still, their mission is to take it out. They don't always wait on Sheriff Richards from Buchanan. They do it with or without him."

"Let's keep these newspapers. We've never known anyone to be in the newspaper much less have a next-door neighbor in the headlines every day. Don't throw them out. There's a trunk in the storage room. Stack them there." With that he folded the ones on the end table and stacked them, then turned to his wife.

"I hate liquor about as much as anyone. When Harry came in drunk and I think about what happened to him, I'll always see the stupidity of liquor," Bingham said to Melviney.

Arreda just could not stand it anymore. She came down the stairway and into the parlor and asked, "Who is Harry? And what happened to him?"

"Oh, Honey. That was a long time ago. You don't need to know terrible things like that." Bingham looked at his wife.

"She's old enough to know. Tell her all about it," Melviney said.

Her daddy pulled a chair out for her to sit close to him. Bingham was a tall, big man with red thinning hair streaked with grey and a big, red-turning-grey handlebar mustache. Arreda loved being close to her daddy. He smelled of leather and sweet pipe tobacco.

"Harry was my older brother. Your Uncle Harry. He came in drunk one night and tried to get a fire going in the pot-bellied stove. Got mad and kicked the stove. He broke his big toe. But just ignored it. Gangrene set in and Dr. Eaves, a young doctor then, had to amputate the toe. Then the foot. Then his leg. He died from gangrene. All because he kicked the stove. Drunk. He was always drunk. That's why he didn't feel the pain. That's why he didn't go to the doctor in spite of what Omega told him to do. He was only 45.

"Just to know all that could have been prevented, and he could have lived a normal, full life. His was another life lost to the use of alcohol. That's why I hate liquor so much. But I'm not out to destroy stills and bring bootleggers to justice. That's what law enforcement is about."

Bingham continued reminiscing, informing his daughter of stories from the past, "Well, I'll tell you about my daddy, but first I'll tell you about Alpha and Omega's daddy.

"Alpha and Omega's daddy died in a prison camp in Elmira, New York during the War Between the States.

"Is he the one who sent Alpha and Omega the rings?"

"He had been home on furlough. Had to go back. It was Civil War times. Then the twins were born. His wife wrote him about the twins. He carved each a ring out of a brass Spencer Carbine shell while he was in prison. He managed to send these tiny rings to her and she gave them to the girls when they were about ten—for their birthday. Alpha lost hers out by the well.

"Oh! That's why she is always going back to the old homeplace looking around in the yard."

"Alpha and Omega are twins, you know, of course. Their mother knew her husband might not make it home and she vowed to never marry again. So she named her daughters, Alpha and Omega—the beginning and the end.

"But she did marry again and had my brother Harry, then me," Jackson Bingham told Arreda with a laugh and a nudge. She just could not make it back then—alone and with two small babies. So after a few years of struggle, she married my father, Jackon Bingham, Sr. I'm Jackson Bingham, Jr.

"Since our mother died and they had to come to live with us, the extra work load of having two more adults in the family has been difficult on Melviney. I know she is always telling you to do things for Alpha and Omega, but then they are also a great help at times. At church, people think they are the grandest thing—twins. They really love church and the people there."

Melviney repeated their names to Arreda who listened attentively, "Christine Alpha and Charlotte Omega. It's very rare for twins to live as long as they have. They will be 60 on their next birthday."

Bootleggers Visit the Parsonage in Draketown

One Saturday evening in the late spring a group of about eight rough-looking men came to Draketown, in a new automobile. They drove slowly through the town looking at each house, searching for the parsonage.

As they drove slowly passed the line of stores, one called out to an old man going into Reeves' Mercantile, "Is that two story house right yonder the parsonage?"

The man on the sidewalk pointed, "Yep. Sure is. That's the parsonage."

They parked the car on the edge of the dirt road. All the men got out and went to the door.

Alice was inside washing the supper dishes; Lorene was playing on the kitchen floor with her kitten; Bob was in his study in the back of the house; Tannie was upstairs. Suddenly there was loud knocking at the door. Alice answered the door and Lorene followed her to see who was doing all that noisy banging. Alice immediately felt fear as she looked into the faces of these eight men. They were unshaven and their clothes were dirty—like they had been in the woods for a while. They all smelled of strong drink.

The man looking her in the eyes, demanded, "We're here to see the pastor."

Lorene hid behind her mother's skirt in fear of this loud-talking, dirty-looking man.

Alice steaded herself, kept looking this one in the eyes, and called out "Bob!"

He came to the door immediately; she took Lorene and stepped back into the room away from the men.

"You're Reverend Stewart," one man spoke loudly in a commanding voice.

The preacher nodded, but kept eye contact. The pastor was rather a small, short man and these men were tall and rough looking.

"We're here to warn you! You been knocking down our stills! That's the only way we got to make a living! We depend on that money! Leave us alone! That's not your job. We're not gonna stop making liquor, no matter how many stills you tear up. You can preach against us and our liquor all you want on Sunday. If the Sheriff catches up with us—that's his job. It's not your job. Leave us alone or you and your family will be sorry," the man reiterated.

When the men left, Alice collapsed on the sofa, shaking. She ventured, "He's right you know."

This angered the pastor more, it seemed, than what the man had said—her taking the men's side.

"I'm doing the Lord's work! I hate liquor, and I love the Lord. It's my calling in this life to fight for all I'm worth to remove it and its temptations from this earth as long as I'm here. I've been fighting whisky making and the evil it causes mankind for a decade," Robert was almost shouting. Lorene ran up the stairway to Tannie.

He was angry about what had happened, but was taking it out on Alice. She remained quiet and listened to him reestablish to her and to himself the basis for his mission—to serve God.

Tannie had been in her bedroom and heard the men beating on the door. She looked out and recognized three of the men but remained there in fear. After the men left she heard the confrontation between her parents. When that subsided, she came into the front room. Lorene sat on the steps of the stairway, listening.

"Daddy. I'm sorry, but I agree with Mama. I've been worried. These men are angry. They are capable of harming us. This is dangerous. Don't you see that? You've got to think of us. I haven't had a chance to tell you, but when I was up at Carroll's store last Saturday, I heard the words, "preacher's daughter" as I as leaving. I glanced around and saw three men standing together inside the door, close as though they were having a confidential conversation."

"All the way from the store, I felt as though someone was watching me. When I turned to come into the yard, I glanced back and saw those same three men on the outside of the store. They were standing close to each other as though they were talking quietly so no one else would hear them.

"Just now when these men knocked on the door, I looked out my window and sure enough, those three men were among this group. They were the ones, and I think they were planning on coming here then. If they are threatening us, we should heed. That's all I'm saying."

The pastor lit into Tannie. "Young lady. First you should have told me about the men before now."

"Daddy, I tried. But you always have people—men and women coming through here day and night. That lady from church who comes here for counseling is always here taking up your time."

Preacher Bob reprimanded his daughter. "Tannie, I have to do the Lord's work. No matter what. I suggest you don't worry. This is not your concern anyway."

She left the room angry and went back to her bedroom. Lorene took her kitten and went to her room. In just a moment, Tannie could be heard playing the fiddle furiously—*Cotton-Eyed Joe*, and stomping her foot on the floor above them to the staccato beat.

All that spring, the pastor and his supporting church members continued their mission to search out and destroy as many stills as they could find. The moonshiners' visit to the parsonage and their threats had not stopped Reverend Stewart; he continued in his relentless quest to spread the gospel against these men and their popular homemade sin.

Dr. Eaves Patches Up Two Drunks

About two weeks later, Dr. Eaves and his wife were both sound asleep in the dark hours past midnight. She nudged him and said, "Did you hear that?"

He listened for a while and said, "Oh, just go back to sleep." He pulled the cover over his head hoping that whatever or whoever it was would go away. BANG! He and his wife sat straight up in bed. He pulled on his pants and shirt, and slipped on his shoes, all of which he had learned to keep ready beside the bed. He lit a lamp, held it to the window, and saw Henry Hicksley pulling Taylor Collins up the front porch steps. Jim Hill was still in the yard leaning against the truck.

Eaves headed to the front door where there were sounds like the door was being bombarded hard enough to bring it down. 'Oh boy. Three drunks. Here we go,' he thought.' When he opened the door, Hicksley and Collins both fell into the room, landing in a pile on the floor.

"What do we have here?" Eaves said as he evaluated the situation. Collins' foot was bleeding because he'd shot himself while Hicksley was getting out of the truck. Collins was hollering something awful. "I dropped my gun! It went off! I'm hit in the foot!"

Eaves helped Collins to the one room set aside to treat patients after hours—like now. When Eaves opened the door, a strong smell of alcohol filled this "patient-treating room" in his house which was located behind his regular office. The lamp he brought into the room illuminated a clean sterile environment, a treatment table in the center, and a medicine cabinet and shelves of equipment on the wall.

While Eaves reached for his medical instruments, Collins lay down on the treatment table. Hicksley brought in Jim Hill, who was bleeding profusely. Hicksley allowed him to collapse on the floor.

Doc thought, 'I'll allow that.' Obviously there had been a fight among these liquor makers. Knives were involved and therefore some gashes and deep cuts and a lot of bleeding resulted. Collins, who lay on the table, started mumbling about a friendly little card game. Doc looked over and said, "You'll have to wait."

Dr. B. F. Eaves & wife Nettie Virginia Frazer Eaves
Courtesy Martha Goldin Church

Then he noticed that Collins also had a gash in his side and blood was oozing there. Collins growled between his pain, "Pete Barber was cheatin' at cards. I accused him."

Eaves got his supplies and knelt on the floor beside Hill who had either gone to sleep or passed out from pain or from spirits. After checking his eyes and seeing a pool of blood on the floor, he rolled him over and looked at the slash on his face, neck, and ear. Hill screamed. Eaves used a cloth to soak up the pool of blood on the floor then started working on him. Hill protested being awakened, being disturbed, and having his wounds cleaned. He hollered, "That hurts; leave me along; let me sleep!"

Eaves told him, "Get yourself under control, or I'll sew your ear back on, backward!"

After giving him ether, Eaves sat on the floor beside him and finished sewing up his face, neck wound, and put the ear back in the correct place. After he finished the stitches, he allowed the man to sleep it off on the floor.

He turned to Collins on the table. There was blood. Lots of blood. After a lot of stitches and a lot of hollering, pain medication, and bandages, he had done all he could for this fellow.

Dr. Eaves got just enough pills from the medicine cabinet for each of the injured men for five days. He tore two pages from the Sears Roebuck catalogue and rolled five pills up in each torn-off sheet.

He turned to Harry Hicksley, gave the folded sheets of the Sears catalogue containing the pills, and told him "One pill a day for each of them, that oughtta do it."

Hicksley paid him handsomely—what this job was really worth. Very few patients paid as well as hurt or injured moonshiners. They had the money. Eaves went back to bed, but slept an uneasy sleep knowing the passed-out, sedated drunk was right there in his home—still sleeping on the floor. When daylight came, Hicksley came back and got him up and out of the house.

Why Stewart Hates Alcohol

One Sunday in June, when the Binghams attended church to hear Reverend Stewart preach, they left the church with a better understanding of why Robert Stewart hated liquor. The pastor was unusually fired up. He "walked the isles" from the front of the church to the back, preaching on the ills of alcohol and on the failings of men to trust in God to deliver them from evil. If he went near the pulpit, you could count on him either hitting the podium with his fist or taking the Bible and holding it in the air and asking God to look down and have mercy on the poor souls who were subject to the evil in this world.

"I have seen tragedy, pain you would not believe, all caused by the drink. I hate the evil. I hate the pain it causes."

The parson grew quiet. He looked at the congregation. Everyone had been at attention, but Arreda was thinking it might be better, right now, not to blink or even to breathe. The pastor was quiet, looking at each person, it seemed like—eye to eye. She felt like he was looking straight at her.

"The worst evil I've seen came when I was just a young man—just a young preacher, just started on the itinerate circuit, in Dahlonega, in 1915." He paused and took a deep breath. It was like he dreaded what he had to say.

"A drunken father came into his house where his wife and children were trying to have a normal life, while he was out drinking. They had an infant son, a few months old. His wife had pulled the living room chair—an overstuffed chair close to the kitchen, and had lain the baby in the chair where she and their four other children were having supper so she could hear the baby if he awoke.

"When her husband came in stumbling, he came toward the kitchen. The wife did not dream he would sit in the big over-stuffed chair. He did. He sat on the poor infant. Crushed its little neck and smothered it with his big drunken body. Then an older child came to get me. Oh the pain and grief I saw, I cannot tell you."

At this point, the pastor had tears in his eyes.

"That's why I hate liquor of any form. I've seen the evil it does," he professed in a booming voice as he hit his fist against the pulpit and glared at the congregation.

Arreda realized her face was wet with tears. She looked around. Her mother was crying. Even her big, red-headed father had tears down to his red-grey mustache. Everyone in the church was stricken. Her mother grabbed her hand and said, "Jackson, let's go."

There's been a whole lot of living which went on, that people don't need to know and don't want to know.

Chapter 4
Warfare on Bootleggers

November 1988

When Arreda told Trisha this story at the beauty shop in Villa Rica, she added, "I'll never forget this tragedy of the drunk sitting on his infant son, Preacher Bob told us about that Sunday. I'll never forget how mother and I cried on the way home. My dad just drove, but he was quiet all the way home."

"Arreda, would you want to come on a Friday? I'm not as busy on Friday, we can still go to the cafe to have lunch, and I won't have to hurry back to the beauty shop.

"Oh, that will be fine. Same time, but next Friday."

The next week, when Arreda came in she said, "I want to tell you what I had heard about these poor, honest Draketown farmers and how they got involved in making moonshine."

A lady approached them, just as Trisha was combing out Arreda's wet hair. "Did you say Draketown? That's where I'm from—at least that's where I was raised.

Arreda said, "I know you. You're Oss Carroll's daughter, Audie Carroll. I haven't seen you in ages."

"Yes. That me. And I recognize you—you're Arreda Bingham. We were in the same class at the Common School back in the 1920s."

Audie was having her hair done at the next booth. For the next hour, Arreda held Audie and Trisha spellbound. Audie even went to lunch with them and was able to add what her dad had told her, about the old days.

The winter of '23-'24 had been hard because of the poor yield of last year's crops. No money. Very little dried or canned food had been put up to aid in getting through the winter months.

The poor farmers handled it in different ways. Most families raised chickens for the eggs and killed maybe one chicken a week to eat, usually for Sunday dinner. As they killed the adult chickens, they raised the baby chickens to take their place.

Late fall and winter gardens helped and could be grown as late as November—with some cabbages, turnips and greens; maybe some onions.

Some farmers sold possessions: One farmer sold an old mule, another sold one of his cows. Some sold their equipment.

But a group of men who were "making it," literally, were making moonshine and driving it over the state line to sell. The money they made from bootlegging was spent on produce while they were in Alabama. To cover, they came home and sold the produce and had enough left for their family and the profit went for new clothes for their children. They quietly took their children to one of the three general mercantile stores in Draketown and bought each a pair of shoes and one outfit of clothes. At first, they did not want to draw attention to their sudden prosperity.

Successful moonshiners, trippers, and bootleggers continued to live in the worn-out farmhouses, and if they had a vehicle, they hid it out of sight: behind the house, in the barn and some built car houses with double doors to close and lock. They stored their whisky making ingredients—mash, cornmeal and sugar sometimes in the car house or in the barn under the hay until it could be picked up and taken to the still.

The only money in circulation seemed to be from moonshiners. Even the store owners were strapped for cash. They often dealt in barter.

"Yes, I'll take your eggs in trade for flour and cornmeal."

"I'll take a mess of turnips and greens in exchange for sugar or coffee," seemed to be the conversation all day long at each of the Draketown Mercantile and Dry Good stores.

Each whisky maker told a brother-in-law or close neighbor what they were doing. Maybe it was that he needed an extra hand at his secret still and maybe he needed an extra hand driving the shine in the night.

To make likker, you needed a creek. Frog Creek, originating in the Appalachian Mountains, came out of the hills of north Georgia and crossed the main road near Yorkville and meandered into Haralson County and crossed Temple Road below Draketown.

The view on any early morning was fog blending with the steam rising from this wide creek; this combination of fog and steam blended with the smoke which trailed upward from many stills set up in the high hills, situated there by the moonshiners to use cold water from this stream. The days were usually clear of smoke, but with the purple haze of twilight, the fires under the big kettles resumed 'til morning.

If revenuers were smart, they could just follow the stream, look for the smoke trails rising upward, track it down, and thar'd be the still.

The ring of whisky makers grew and their activities picked up after dark. In the summer, a loaded vehicle could not travel until after nine o'clock in the evening. Many residents were sitting on their porch until after nine enjoying a cool breeze, listening to the katydids, night sounds, and watching their children playing outside, chasing fire flies. These summer nighttime activities kept moonshiners waiting. After they were sure everyone had gone in, the trippers, with car lights off, would ease out of town; a scattering of residents might notice the noise of a motorcar passing.

Toby Howard

Toby Howard and his wife, Mollie, and their six children had enjoyed a nice Thanksgiving and survived the winter, existing on the hog meat he had been given for helping Mr. Cole kill a couple more hogs. Cole paid in the hog meat of course. With the few chickens, they had eggs. And there had been the winter garden—until it had frozen solid. About January, Toby knew he had to do something.

He had gone up the hill to his cousin's on-going still and joined them. They were eager to have an extra hand. They taught him what he needed to know.

His Uncle James Hendrix said, "Here's a test. Pour a small amount of likker into a spoon, set it on fire, and watch to see the color as it burns. If it burns a blue flame, it's safe; if it burns a yellow flame, it's tainted; if it burns a reddish flame, there's lead in it. There's a saying, '*lead turns it red and makes you dead.*' So stay away from radiators when you distill—they contain lead."

After the first week, he was given one fifth of the "take." They were able to make more liquor than they had been now that they had an extra man who actually lived closer to their still. They split the "take" five ways—four at the still and one driving the shine to Alabama—about fifty miles west.

When Toby came home with seventy-five dollars, he planned to spend this money where it counted the most. He didn't tell his wife or let on to his sons. He headed up to Draketown to Oss Carroll's store. There, with his hands shaking in excitement and thankfulness, but also with a little fear that someone would ask him where he got so much money, he paid off his debt and began his purchases. He bought cheese, bacon, syrup, flour for biscuits and pies, cornmeal for cornbread, canned peaches and homemade canned goods. He went to George Hudson and bought a couple of laying chickens and a couple more to eat.

That night at home, Mollie cooked up the best supper they had had since December.

The next morning, Mollie cooked bacon, made biscuits, and put the Karo syrup on the table. The children were delighted. Each spent time putting a pat of butter into the puddle of dark syrup on their plate and mixing it with a knife then dragging the hot biscuit through the mixture.

Sandy, the oldest, asked, "Mama, can I have another biscuit to sop up the syrup? And can I have more syrup?"

When she passed the plate, Gene said with a happy eagerness, "Me to," as he reached to help himself. The Karo was passed around a couple of times. When Mollie fed the baby the soft buttered crumbs dipped in the sweet syrup, she ate an entire biscuit.

After that first week, Toby was in. If this is what it took to live like a man—taking care of his family, that's what he would become—a moonshiner.

Toby worked on Frog Creek for his Uncle James Hendrix and his cousins, Owen and Hubert, all of 1924.

He was careful to spend his new income on just what he needed without becoming extravagant and drawing attention. He spent most of the money on food and clothes. His children started back to school now that they had decent clothes. The money he had left each week—his wife hid it in a jar buried in the back corner of the barn.

When his oldest son, Sandy, cut his foot, Toby was able to take him to Dr. Eaves to get stitches and was proud that he could pay. Toby was starting to gain a little pride now that his overalls were new and not the dirty thread-bare ones he usually took off to wash on Saturdays. He had even begun to think about taking his children to church now that his wife could dress them decently.

One late spring day, Mollie walked the mile to Draketown for a shopping trip. She bought several pieces of printed cotton fabric and a pattern and went to the Alpha

& Omega Dressmakers to have them sew a couple of spring and summer dresses for her. While in Draketown, she had her long hair cut into a short bob at the local barber, who cut both men's and women's hair.

Toby hardly recognized her when she came back into the farmhouse that night. She was beaming and looked years younger. She was also carrying a bag of groceries and one of clothes for the younger children. Life seemed good for Toby and Mollie and their family in the summer of 1924, better than since they first married.

George Hudson, Innovator

George Hudson, a farmer-turned-moonshiner, drove his old T-Model truck early in the morning, supposedly loaded down with eggs through town as though he were going to market in Buchanan. Under the top layer of eggs were gallons of whisky—headed for Alabama. He took a path close to the Phillips' farm into the thick woods, where he met some of the gang who transferred the whisky to their car. They paid him. He sat where waiting for hours for the time to pass. He had his dinner and plenty of water and waited in the shade.

When it was about the time that he would have returned from Buchanan, a trip which took most of the day, he went home with an empty truck, a roll of money in his pocket, and a smug feeling of hope and excitement. He was up the next morning, ready to make more whisky.

Most residents went to bed by dark. If you didn't, you had to buy kerosene that you could not afford for the lamps. One rarely burned a lamp at night.

One night, a lamp burned in the window of the Bingham house. Omega was ill; Melviney and Jackson Bingham were trying to decide what to do and if they should call Dr. Hogue, from across the street. Jackson glanced out the window and saw a motorcar go slowly down the dirt street in front of the house. He went down the hall to the front room and looked at the clock over the mantel. Three o'clock. What was anyone doing out this time of night?

Bingham did phone Dr. Hogue. When the doctor came and attended to Omega, he found that her heart was weak.

"She never really got over having the influenza back in 1918, during the time of the epidemic. It's lucky that she even survived it. So many didn't." Dr. Hogue told Jackson who nodded in understanding.

"You remember our mother, Era, did not survive," Jackson said with a far away look in his eyes.

"I remember Dr. Eaves was in attendance to Omega and Era. That was the busiest I had ever been. The whole country was affected and many lives were lost."

"Era was 74 and Omega was 54. That was six years ago. We've been through some hard times," Jackson reminisced.

Melviney came into the room to check on Omega. She looked at Dr. Hogue then went over to ask questions.

"Keep her in bed and feed her only broth and water," Hogue told Melviney. "Keep her as comfortable as possible. She just needs a good rest. She'll probably be all right in a couple of days."

Bingham walked Dr. Hogue to the front porch. A little light shone from her bedroom to the porch while the two men conversed.

"Dr. Hogue, I'm sorry I had to call you at this hour." At that moment another automobile went slowly down the street.

Both men stopped talking, looked at the passing car. "There goes the night-riders," Bingham said. They both may have known what was going on, but each was thinking of Omega at that time.

About a month later, George Hudson, the farmer-turned-moonshiner who covered his load of moonshine with eggs, realized he needed help to fill his orders of whisky. He recruited his brother-in-law, Clyde Barber, who had lost his wife earlier in the year. Clyde said he would help if he were needed, but he wanted no part in making the whisky. Hudson took Barber with him to his still behind a shed in his backyard in plain sight of the scattering of small houses on the edge of Draketown.

Barber was shocked. "Aren't you afraid you'll be seen here. This is illegal."

"There's nothing like being right under the nose of the law. I only cook the mash at night or when my wife does her wash. The smoke from the wood fire under the boiler of whisky could be mistaken for the smoking fire when my wife boils the clothes when she washes."

Hudson had built a plain wood structure around the big pot with the coil so it could be mistaken for another chicken house. He bought another 100 chicks from the feed store in Buchanan and added enough fence to accommodate these growing hens. The mash he bought was not chicken feed, but used to make moonshine. To the casual observer, this set up appeared like a farmer raising chickens, having eggs to sell, with an industrious wife who washed more than one day a week!

With Barber helping Hudson with his "chicken business," his job was to drive the car load of whisky that was topped with chicken eggs down the road at least three mornings a week—Monday, Wednesday and Friday—like he was going to market in Buchanan. Barber was to wait for the car from Alabama and the whisky-runners in broad daylight, down the dirt path by the Phillips' farm. The men from Alabama arrived, paid Barber a roll of money, loaded the moonshine into their vehicle and left him on the dirt path in the thick woods to wait until time to return to Draketown.

Barber sat in the car in the shadows of the pines around him, with the roll of money in his hand. He was almost afraid to open it and count it. It felt so wrong to be doing this. But after a few minutes, he counted the bills. $200. More than he had seen at one time in his entire life. As he counted it again, he began to feel hope for the first time since before Naomi died leaving him with three children to raise.

His part was $50. Just to bring the truck loaded with eggs and whisky to the dirt path, wait for it to be picked up, wait until late in the day, and then to return to Draketown. This freed up George Hudson to make more moonshine while he was gone.

After the second week, they realized that Barber needed to make a mid-week run of eggs to market. For the few eggs he brought back to Draketown under the tarp, there eventually was a build-up of eggs.

On Wednesday, Barber left Draketown as usual about 8:00 a.m. headed to Buchanan to the market to sell Hudson's eggs. Hudson had put a couple of his mature chickens, in wire crates, to sell also. As Barber neared the path turn-off to Phillips' farm, a car came toward him. He was shocked and his hands began to tremble as he recognized it to be the sheriff's vehicle. The sheriff motioned for him to pull over. He pulled to the side of the road.

Sheriff George Richards stepped out of his vehicle. "Barber! You been going to market three times a week. We've been watching Hudson's chicken farm. You leave Draketown with a load, but you're never seen at the market. There's something wrong about this."

Barber managed to mumble, "Hudson hired me to take these eggs and chickens to market. That's what I do."

Hudson had told Barber that if he were ever caught or accused of anything not to admit to anything—act totally innocent. So that's what he did. He put this surprised look on his face. This was easy to do. He tried to hide his trembling fingers by gripping the steering-wheel of the truck.

Without a warrant to search, Sheriff Richards went to the back of the truck, took off the crates of live chickens on each side of the bed of the truck and jerked the tarp off the center of the truck. There in neat rows were twelve dozen eggs—all that Hudson's chicken had laid since last Wednesday. The Sheriff just kept staring at the eggs. He took a few off and put them back carefully in the row. Then he tilted a couple of crates up and saw the line of eggs, some white, some brown. For a few minutes, Sheriff Richards said nothing. The deputy who had rode with him, got out of the car and came to the back of the truck. The deputy looked under the truckbed and went through the eggs, also.

The sheriff told him, "Careful, don't break the eggs. There's nothing wrong here." The sheriff nodded to Barber to be on his way, but he sat there and waited for their automobile to clear, then he continued to Buchanan with his load of chickens and eggs.

Late that day, Barber was back in Draketown. He took the truck back to Hudson. When he unloaded the crates, he had placed the money he had gotten for the eggs at Buchanan market in one of the crates and did not hand it to Hudson. When Hudson saw the money in the crate, he jerked his head around in question.

"Sheriff Richards pulled me over, searched the back of the truck and when he found nothing suspicious, let me go. This is my last trip. I kept quiet and acted innocent like you told me to do. I'm saying this is my last trip. Your chicken farm is being watched. Do what you want, but leave me out of it."

With that Barber was gone and out of the moonshine business, at least for a while.

In the middle of the night that same Wednesday, the chicken house was raided by the Sheriff and two deputies. They expected to surprise Hudson in the act of operating a liquor still. But to their chagrin, they only found a hundred baby chicks. Hudson heard the cars and the commotion, but did not go outside. He knew he had already gotten rid of any evidence of a still. He had already moved it to a creek close to one of the old copper mines in the hills north of Draketown.

Barber and His $350

Clyde and his seven-year-old daughter, Janice, looked after the new baby when they were each home. If he left the house and Janice and Johnny were in school, he could trust Telma to feed little Clyde Junior and to change him. But when he came home, he went straight to check on his son, making sure he was clean and had been fed.

Now that Clyde was out of the bootlegging business, he was anxious and relieved at the same time. He had been a bootlegger for two weeks and a day, almost got caught, then quit the business. But he had the $350 Hudson paid him.

Now that Clyde had money, he went to see Dr. Eaves, "What can be done for Junior? He is two months old, but so small and pale and listless."

Dr. Eaves replied, "Well, he needs the kind of care only a new mother can give him. I don't know of anyone here in Draketown. There's a new mother over near Yorkville, but she is not strong enough for two babies. You might check with Tamammy. I know how connected your two families have been in the past. She might know someone who would help you out."

Clyde rode his horse down the narrow, winding road a mile or so past the grist mill to Mud Creek Road to find Tamammy, the oldest negro woman in the community. She was sitting on the porch in the warm May sunshine. She set up quickly in her chair, surprised to see a white man coming toward her house.

He called out to her, "Tamammy. It's Clyde Barber."

"Well Lord Have Mercy!" I ain't seen you in years. Heard about your precious wife a'dying. The Lord's got another angel up there in heaven. I know that's true, for sure."

"Tamammy, that's why I'm here. I need help and knew you would find what I need. My son, Junior, his health is poorly. I need a wet nurse. Is there anyone here who would take him. I can pay. I can pay good."

With that, her eyes caught a sparkle.

"My granddaughter's a'nursing her little son. She will do it. I know she will."

With saying that, Tamammy, screamed, "Merilou! Merilou!"

In just a minute, a young strong-looking woman peered out the window of the house next door.

"Big Mama, what you want?" Then Merilou saw the tall, white man on the porch and came over to stare at him from the narrow yard that separated the two weather-boarded, tiny old houses. She carried a handsome, brown child on her hip who looked to be several months old.

"Merilou, this here man has a business proposition for you." Merilou regarded

Clyde with mild curiosity.

Clyde turned to her, "I need a wet-nurse for my infant son. He is faring poorly and I think nursing would put some life into him. My wife died. I can pay you $2 a week to take him for several months."

Somewhere between the words "my wife died" and "I can pay you $2 a week," Merilou's demeanor changed from mild curiosity to intense sympathy and high interest.

"I'll take that baby and make him strong as mine," she glanced at her son and looked at Clyde with a determined promise in her bright, eager eyes.

Clyde stayed a moment to remember their families' past with Tamammy.

"Son, I'll do anything for you and your family. Your Grandpap Barber sure was good to us back when I was a child. After the 'Mancipation Proclamation, he said we were free to go or to stay and work on his farm and get paid. That's what my Mama and me did. He was always kind to us. Everyone else left the farm to go out on their own. Mama said we know what we got here. She was afraid to leave. We spent our days looking after your Granpap. He came back from that war a cripple, you know. When he died, a couple years back, was like my own kin was gone."

"That son of his never turned out too good." As she said this she realized she was talking about Clyde's daddy, Oscar. She started to apologize but asked, "You ever hear what happened to him when he just walked off and left the mule and plow right there in the middle of the field?"

"We got a letter from a relative in Alabama. Seems he found a woman and married her. He's living over in Alabama unless he got tired of her and walked off again." They both tried to laugh a little.

Clyde rode the horse back to the house and told Telma, "I've found a wet-nurse for Junior. I'm paying her two dollars a week to keep him and take care of him."

He asked Telma to bundle up Junior's blankets and clothes. She was not happy. She argued, "I'm aga'n' it. I'm taking good care of yor'n baby. I'm doing the best I can. Why didn't you pay me two dollars a week?"

Clyde put Junior's things in a bag, mounted the horse, and reached down to take the baby from Telma. She relented and handed the bundle-of-a-baby up to him.

"I'm aga'n' it. I'm aga'n' it!" Telma followed the horse and rider, who held the baby, to the edge of the yard.

She screamed, "I'm aga'n' it," which echoed over the hill and back to her. She stood watching until the horse and rider were out of sight.

When Clyde returned home, Janice and Johnny had come in from school while he was at Merilou's. They took it hard that their baby brother was not there.

"I miss him," whined Janice as she clung to Clyde.

"Come here young lady." He sat on a low chair and pulled Janice toward him in a big bear hug. Clyde explained that Merilou could feed Junior and this would help him get strong and healthy.

"We'll go visit him next week. After he is old enough to eat on his own, we'll get him back to live with us."

After the children were consoled a bit, Clyde surprised them when he said, "I would like to buy something for you. Anything you want. Think about it and tell me."

"I want something for Mommy. I want her to have a tombstone." I saw the nice tombstones the day of her funeral," Janice said.

Johnny interrupted. "I want marbles." Clyde responded by reaching out to Johnny and drawing him into a bear hug also and saying, "You will get a bag of marbles. I'll take you with me to Reeves, pay off some debt, and buy a bag of marbles for you."

When Johnny said marbles, that reminded Janice of the nicer tombstones, "I want a marble tombstone for Mommie."

"Well now. I have a lot to buy, I don't think we can spend all our money on a tombstone. But I will see what I can do."

The next day the three of them went to Reeves' Mercantile, getting what they needed. When they reached the cemetery, Clyde made a wooden frame from old boards he had torn off an old shed out back of their farmhouse. Clyde used the wood to frame the grave. He mixed the cement with the water he had brought in a big bucket and poured concrete to make a slab over the grave.

In the process, Johnny, playing near by, shot a marble across the sandy ground and it fell into the cement and stuck. For an instant, they froze, horror-struck that Johnny had messed up the precious tombstone. Janice opened her mouth to reprimand her little brother.

Then they remained quiet for a second and all at once said together, "Hey, that's a marble tombstone."

They laughed, and each set about selecting just the right color marbles to decorate the wet slab of concrete.

They hurried back to Reeves' and bought three more bags: two more for the wet cement slab and one for Johnny. The three of them excitedly hurried back to the cemetery and finished placing colorful marbles all over the wet slab before it hardened.

At the end of this early summer day in the fading light, they walked home. Janice turned to look back every few steps. They thought Naomi's was the most beautiful marble tombstone in the cemetery—like no other. With a sharpened stick, Clyde had scratched in the cement, "Naomi Barber—wife, mother 1900—1924."

Clyde Barber Goes Back to Bootlegging

Several days after he left Junior with Merilou, Clyde lay at night on the bed, covered by the homemade quilt Naomi made him. He was cozy and warm, thinking about Junior, missing him. Had he done the right thing leaving the baby with Merilou?

His thoughts returned to this world, to his children, his mother, and the farm. He had bought Janice and Johnny some clothes at Oss Carroll's store. He had bought Telma clothes also and paid off the debt at the bank and at the store. He bought the staples they needed: coffee, sugar, flour and bacon. It had been a long time since they had killed a hog; having bacon was like old times. What was he going to do for money now? He had promised to pay Merilou $2 a week. He had at least $2 left for her first week, but nothing to pay her next week.

Early the next morning after he got Johnny and Janice off to school, Clyde saddled the horse, mounted, and turned it toward his cousin's farm. About a half-hour later, he was at Pete Barber's old house. Pete's dad, Charles Barber, was his daddy's brother. Oscar Barber was Charles Barber's older brother.

The fields were unplowed, the porch needed repair, the yard was covered in tall weeds, but beside the house was a 1923 Ford T-Model automobile.

Pete came out on the porch, still in his nightshirt, "What the hell? Cousin, what are you doing way over here? Come on in."

Clyde dismounted, left the horse hitched to the post in the front yard, and followed Pete into the kitchen where he was already pouring each of them a cup of coffee.

"I'm ready to take you up on the offer you made me after Naomi's funeral. I'll be a tripper. Just to Atlanta. I have to think of my family and not leave them—long. I'll do two runs a week— two trips into Atlanta a week. No more. That's all. And I prefer to take night runs."

"Hold on, slow down. You're all wound up. We'll figure this out. I can let you use my car. I have it designed to hold at least one-hundred gallons. We'll take it out one night and I'll show you how to slide into the side roads if you're being chased by revenuers. I want you to transport likker into Atlanta, and bring back the bushel bags of sugar and cornmeal.

Clyde pulled his cane-bottom straight chair closer to the table and slumped down to do a little planning while he slowly sipped the steaming black coffee. He had a far away look in his eyes. His heart was beating fast with excitement and maybe a little hope, tinged with fear. He sighed and hoped he would not regret what he was planning to do.

Pete went into the bedroom, dressed, and continued to tell him the details of moonshining, "Buying corn meal from Cissero Bishop at his grist meal up in Draketown would raise too much suspicion. Anyway we can buy corn meal cheaper, for seventy cents a bushel. It comes in two-bushel sacks. We buy 100 bushel, fifty two-bushel sacks. We keep a stash. I have it hidden out in the barn under the hay. You can't grow corn and have it ground that cheap. That's the way it works if you buy it in bulk. The contacts are set up in Atlanta."

Pete came out of the bedroom, pulled on a coat, and they were out the front door, and in a few minutes they were in the barn. Pete showed him in the T-Model where the moonshine was stored for transport into Atlanta. "Here's where you put the bushel bags of corn meal and sugar to bring back."

Pete continued, "We get three gallons of liquor to a bushel of cornmeal. We take five 100 pound sacks of sugar and ten bushels of cornmeal and make fifty gallons of whisky—ten gallons out of every sack of sugar, maybe more. We use brown sugar; it's cheaper. We pay $3 to $3.75 for a 100 pound sack of sugar. We get $2.00 for a gallon of white lightning. That triples the money we paid for sugar and cornmeal.

"Several of us boys, have a fifty-gallon still on the side of Frog Mountain—the creek feeds down from that mountain and provides the still with fresh clean water. Pete paused. You remember my younger brother, Tom—he's helping some. Dropped out of school last year. Said farming's not for him. There are no jobs. So, he's helping me now."

"I didn't realize your younger brother was old enough for things like this. I remember him as just a kid."

"Well, he's grown up to be a big guy. Can do a day's work like any man, when he wants to, when there's something to be gained. Like cash," Pete filled him in and let out with a big laugh when he said cash.

Clyde cautioned, "I don't want to make any likker. But I'll do the runs at night, into Atlanta."

"While we're here, I better feed the animals." Pete stayed at the barn for chores and Clyde walked back and sat on the porch waiting for him. As he sat there he thought back. He did not entirely trust his cousin, Pete. When they were together as boys at their Grandpap Barber's farm, they always got into trouble when they were really just trying to have fun. First time, they tried to ride the cow and scared it so bad, Grandpap said it didn't give milk for two days. Another time they tried to ride a young mare that wasn't old enough to be ridden.

Grandpap Barber came limping out of the house with his cane, hollering, "Get off that mare! You're going to injure her back. She's not old enough to ride!"

By the time Grandpap reached them, they were off. He grabbed both the boys by their shirt collars, and looked each one of them in the eyes. "When you two come to visit, you are to leave the livestock alone. I mean it. You won't know what a tanning-on-your-backside is until I get through with you."

On a rainy summer day when they were at Grandpap's farm, neither of them thought they could get into trouble. Neither did Grandpap. Pete had his little terrier dog with him. The boys decided they would visit the barn and see what was there. Soon they decided to turn each bale of hay over to see if they could find a rat.

A few times, a rat did come scurrying out; then, they sicced the dog on it. Soon the commotion and hollering and barking that came from the barn brought Pap struggling to run with his cane down the hill from the house in the rain with a black slicker thrown over his head. He stood just inside the doorway being partly pelted with a torrent of rain for a few seconds, watching the boys who were unaware of his presence. He decided to join the fun; he grabbed the pitch fork, and tried to eliminate a few of the scurrying critters. He would not allow the boys to use the pitchfork. They had a howling time of it that all ended in a great deal of laughter.

After Pete and Clyde turned fifteen, Pete turned mean, ornery and Clyde suspected, started breaking the law. What they had done as kids was mischief; what Pete did later, was criminal.

One summer when they were fifteen, Clyde noticed that Pete had a shiny new knife and questioned, "Where'd you get that ?"

"Oh, up at Oss Carroll's store," he grinned big as he replied.

Clyde asked, "But did you pay for it?" Pete's sly grin widened and he didn't answer.

It was about this time that Clyde's dad disappeared, leaving his family when he walked off and left the mule and plow in the field. He did not have time to see Pete much after that. Clyde was too busy trying to be the man of the house and run the farm. Clyde suspected that Pete had a mean streak—maybe of pure evilness —one put there by poverty and hardness. The older he got, the more vindicative he became. But in this situation, Clyde needed Pete to show him the ins and outs of the whisky business. He needed money.

Pete came back from the barn and the two of them went inside, where Pete continued to inform, "Now Cousin, you need to know some things, and I will educate you. You know, cotton used to be king around here, but now corn whisky is king around these parts. We try for a three days turn-around time for a batch. That's what it takes to fill the orders we have waiting. We mix twenty-five pounds of sugar in a barrel with a bushel of cornmeal and add about eight gallons of water from Frog Creek. Here you have clear white lightning," Pete instructed.

"This white lightning looks like water and at first it goes down smooth like water. Then it light up your throat and innards like you just swallowed flaming sugar or a light bulb. It's about 125-150 proof. We water it down, called cutting. That brings it down to 98-100 proof. Advice to a first timer taking a swig is just to go ahead and sit down on the floor and lean up against a wall 'cause that's where you'll end up by the time the white lightning hits your stomach."

"Remember 173 degrees. That's where alcohol boils. At this temperature, the steam goes into a coil called a worm. Then you cool it, and it turns back into liquid. That's your likker."

"I told you; I'm not getting involved in making this whisky, just transporting it," Clyde insisted.

Pete continued with the unwanted information. Clyde knew he was just showing off. Pete was trying to impress him with his knowledge of making moonshine, like he was a big shot. He wasn't a big shot; he was just trying to be one. Clyde thought of the new Ford sitting outside. Pete *was* a big-shot moonshiner and bootlegger, he guessed.

Pete was feeling excited to be impressing his cousin. He spouted off: "*A cup of likker, you feel glad; Overdo it, you'll go mad; Drink a bit, often, you'll be wise; Drink too much, it'll forever close your eyes.*"

Pete let out a big wicked laugh and hit Clyde on the shoulder. "Tonight, buddy, I'll take you around."

Trippin' into Atlanta Begins

With Pete's 1923 T-Model Ford, Clyde began making the trip into Atlanta. The first night Pete rode with him, showing him where the contact was located. They drove to a small, dark restaurant on 10th street, parked, went in to an empty restaurant, no customers—just a man, Whitey, waited. They gave him the keys and sat in a booth, having a cup of coffee waiting for him to return.

When Whitey came back, he handed them the keys and an envelope and told them everything was fine. He had driven the car into a nearby warehouse, unloaded it, filled the compartments with corn meal and sugar, drove it back to the restaurant, and parked in front. Pete took the envelope, lowered it out of view, peaked in and saw $500. He slipped Clyde $50 which he put down the inside of his boot. Pete took the remaining $450 and slipped it down inside his boot and gave the empty envelope to Whitey.

Whitey, a tall muscular prematurely white-haired man with white bushy eyebrows, walked over with Clyde to the door then, said in a confidential, secret voice, "See you on Wednesday."

It wasn't a question. It was a command, one that made Clyde a little uneasy. He nodded. Pete and Clyde left. He was quiet as they drove home. He was in. No way to get out of this now. Wednesday and Friday nights were uneventful. So were the three nights the next week. At the end of the second week, Pete bought himself a new 1924 T-Model. It was a larger car. He set about altering it to hold more moonshine and more corn meal and sugar for the return trips. He gave Clyde his 1923 T-Model.

"It's got some miles on it. It's been driven hard and is a little beat-up, but should do you well."

Until now Clyde had just slipped out of the house and was back before the children were up. No one missed him but Telma, who caught him coming in one morning about 3:00 a.m. She gave him the eye. She did not understand what he was doing, but knew going out after bedtime every night and coming in at the wee hours of the morning could not be legal.

When he drove the car home and parked it beside the house, Telma shook her fist at him and asked, suspiciously, "Where'd you get that car?" She used the same tone she would have in accusing him of stealing it.

The kids had a fit. He promised to take them for a ride the next Saturday.

That first night that he had the car and he did not make a run, Clyde lay in bed, thinking of Junior. It had been three weeks and they had only visited him twice. He had a decision to make.

Early the next morning, Clyde drove the car to see Merilou. When he pulled up, Tamammy was at Merilou's house helping her with Ben, her young son, and with Junior. They each looked out the window, surprised to see a car drive up and to see Clyde get out of it.

This warm summer morning he walked into the small house and immediately took his son and held him. Junior was alert and had put on a pound or two. He took him in his arms to the window to see him in the morning light.

"He looks good. I believe his color is better."

He turned to Merilou, who looked apprehensively at him. "It's only been three weeks."

"Yes I know. Here's what I would like to do. I want you to consider coming to live at our house, at least during the day. I can pick you up at 6:00 every morning and bring you back about 8:00 every night. You bring your child and take care of both the babies at my house. We can have enough food for you also."

Merilou looked at Tamammy with a question in her eyes. She wanted to know what her grandmother thought. "I will pay you $5 a week if you stay with us and help get the meals for all of us—me, my mother, Janice, Johnny, you, and also nurse the two babies—your Ben, and Junior," Clyde added.

Tamammy nodded to Merilou, indicating for her to say yes. The babies were soon bundled up and on the way in the car back to the Barber's farmhouse. "I have a room for you and the babies at night if you ever have to stay because of sickness or the weather—if I can't bring you home." Merilou nodded.

Things were going fast for her. "We'll see," is all she would say.

They were back home, parked and went inside as Johnny, Janice, and Telma were getting up. The children were so happy to see little Junior. Telma was the first to take him, and they gathered around to observe how much he had grown.

"I'm picking Merilou up early every morning and she is staying all day; then, I will take her home after everyone is asleep each night." He regarded Telma and could almost see bristles raising up on her like they would on the back of a dog brought into a sudden situation requiring attack.

He added, "Merilou's going to help cook all our meals." It was as though a peaceful blanket was drawn around Telma's demeanor. Now she would have the help she needed around here. Clyde read her thoughts and silently agreed with what she was probably thinking.

"Maw, you'll have to look after the baby at night if he wakes and I'm not here."

Merilou added, "I can leave some milk for you in a crock. You can use a rag." They all knew that a baby could suck on a small rag soaked with milk and could get enough milk to be pacified.

At that moment, Clyde realized he could afford to buy a baby bottle he had heard about if not at Reeves, maybe up in Atlanta. He might go one night when the stores were still open and find a baby bottle with a teat for junior to have available at night. It could be worked out.

Several months after Clyde began trippin' into Atlanta, he bought an older model truck, similar to the one he had driven for George Hudson when he had hauled gallons of liquor in tins covered over with eggs. He gave the 1923 Ford T-Model back to Pete to do whatever he wanted to with it. He would probably give it to his younger brother, Tom.

Clyde had a plan. Jacking the springs of the truck so that when it held 200 pounds of moonshine going into Atlanta and 200 pounds of sugar and cornmeal coming from Atlanta would keep it from looking weighted down. He built a wooden-box, and painted it black so the truck bed appeared empty. He mounted this box over another box underneath which would hold his cargo while coming from and going into Atlanta. Clyde covered the back of the top box with produce that he had grown. For his first trip to Atlanta in this truck, he wore overalls, his field boots, and the old floppy hat he wore when he plowed. He made his runs into Atlanta during the day, driving slowly—going to market loaded with a little produce. In June and July, he managed to grow a little corn, loaded it and headed to market.

When Clyde got into Atlanta, he sold the produce first, then went to the designated restaurant, and gave Whitey his key. Whitey drove the truck into the warehouse where the liquor was unloaded and the sugar and cornmeal were added to the black structure underneath the empty truck bed. Whitey seemed enthusiastic about having day runs. There was less suspicion and therefore less danger of being caught.

To anyone watching, a revenuer or a casual observer, Clyde was a farmer who brought his produce into the Farmer's Market, stopped by an out-of-the-way restaurant, had a quick dinner and drove slowly back to Draketown with the few dollars he got for the produce. He hid extra sugar and cornmeal in his barn underneath the hay bales until Pete got it during the night between 12:00 and 3:00 a.m.

Clyde built a car house behind his house to store this older truck. Those who noticed knew he had a vehicle. It wasn't a secret. But he did not drive around. He only picked up Merilou in the mornings and took her home at night. He farmed in between and took a produce run once a week. If he could not grow enough vegetables to go to market twice a week, then he would resort to a midnight run into Atlanta.

Clyde averaged a hundred dollars a week and was careful how he spent it. He began putting some away. After he paid off all debts, he bought clothes for everyone including Merilou and both babies; then, he became just a hardworking farmer—growing vegetables. He bought a couple of hogs and a new plow.

On the days Clyde did not make a run into Atlanta, he devoted his time to growing corn. Clyde fared better than some by growing his garden and the produce corn on the acre down by Frog Creek—the bottom land grew well having moisture from the creek for irrigation.

Clyde could pick up Merilou and her baby, Ben, at 6:00 a.m., go into Atlanta, leaving by 7:00 a.m. and bringing back a load by 12:00 or 1:00. He spent his afternoon plowing, or pulling fodder and could take Merilou and Ben back by 8:00 p.m.

Everything was going smooth. By September, Junior was six-months old. He was smaller than some babies his age, but his weight and color had improved. Junior seemed a happy baby.

Merilou was happy with the arrangement. Some nights when there was leftover beans or cornpone, Clyde suggested she take that for Tamammy. After all, she was getting on up in age and had relied on Merilou before she went to the Barber's every day.

There was a general agreement that Merilou would stay with the Barbers for the winter. Next March, Junior would be a one-year-old and, by then, he could thrive on soft food from the table.

Meet at the Cotton Gin

The summer of 1924 saw an escalation between the whisky makers and those trying to stop them. The summer's sparse rain brought the worse drought to the South in decades. Haralson, Paulding, and Polk Counties in Northwestern Georgia were so dry the red clay fields broke up into designs of brittleness. There was almost no rain in June, July, and August; crops were "burnt-up." There was nothing to sell; no income for the families to live on until the next harvest—next year.

By the fall of 1924, people were desperate. Most families had a garden, but after a summer of meager rain, these had not produced the food to "put-up," to can and dry for the winter months. Most summer and fall gardens were in a pitiful state.

One August morning, when Melviney was in the garden out behind the house, she grabbed a handful of carrot tops and pulled up carrots the size of her little finger. The tomatoes were half the size they should be, the okra stalks were knee high and produced no okra. The corn stalks grew only chest-high turning brown on the end, bearing miniature ears of corn. Shucking the corn, revealed a tiny cob with just "blisters" instead of mature grains of yellow corn. She drew a bucket of water from the well on the porch and carried it down to the thirsty vegetables when she looked up and saw Jackson and Bud walking past, going to work at the grist mill.

They all looked surprised. "Oh, I thought you two had already gone to work," she straightened up looking at her husband and son from under the brim of her straw hat.

"Melviney, are you totin' water for the garden? It's hopeless in this heat and it's not good for your back," Jackson said putting his hands on his hips in exasperation.

"I've been doing it all summer, otherwise we wouldn't have had anything to eat. That's why we're having only fried green tomato biscuits for supper. But I'm worried about the well. Being that it's so dry now with little rain for the last two month, I was afraid the well might dry up. Then we'd really be in a mess with no water."

"I don't think we have to worry about the well drying up. It goes down probably thirty feet. There's water down there."

Jackson turned to his son, "Bud, you stay and help your mother put a couple of buckets of water on the garden then come on down to the mill."

Everywhere garden yield was small or burnt-up and in the fields farmers saw devastation. Acres of small corn stalks stood browning to brittle all over the countryside. Acres of peas grew low and green, but the pods were flat, never filling out. The rows and rows of vibrant, green alfalfa were planted to plow under to replenish the soil with nutrients. These acres of healthy plants blossomed purple in May, but by August these plants failed to thrive and some died from lack of moisture. More farmers became desperate. More turned to moonshining.

Reverend Robert Stewart intensified his fight against the evils of "these spirits." Stewart was on fire. He and his crew of Christian crime fighters hit stills up and down Frog Creek. Men were angry—and weary. Desperation and violence was reported in local and state newspapers.

Moonshiners were under attack. The Hendrix's stills had been taken down twice by Reverend Stewart and his church members. Toby Howard barely escaped getting caught by revenuers. Clyde Barber's trips into Atlanta came to a stop—no whisky to run. No further income. Pete Barber's family still had been destroyed and several men were taken to jail by revenuers. He and his brother Tom, barely escaped into the woods.

After the local whisky makers and some not-so-locals had run-ins with Stewart, there was talk of a flogging—to teach him a lesson, to make sure he had the message, "Leave the stills alone. These stills provided income for families who needed help."

Late one Saturday night in November, a truck with it lights turned off drove slowly to the parsonage and stopped. The driver and passenger got out, unloaded a wood structure, then carefully and quietly so as not to make any noise, slid this long rectangle, with a lid nailed tight, onto the porch; it was a six foot long coffin with the initials **R S** crudely carved into the top of the lid.

Then the pair of men, moonshiners, ran quickly back to the truck. One moonshiner asked apprehensively, "Does this mean we're going to kill the preacher?"

The driver, who seemed to be in charge, replied, "No. We're just going to scare the living daylights out of him. This is yet another warning for him to leave our stills alone." With that said, they drove off into the dark, cold night.

On Sunday morning, the Stewart family was up early getting ready for church.

Guy Austin, who was Stewart's assistant who had accompanied him on many raids, came up on the porch to visit the preacher and saw the coffin. He knocked quietly; Alice answered the door, saw the coffin, and stepped outside out onto the porch.

She looked confused at first, then the implication slowly came to her and she said quietly, "I'll get Bob. The two of you get rid of this. I don't want my girls seeing it. Lorene won't understand, but Tannie will; she has been terribly upset about this war with the moonshiners since they came to the house last spring."

When Reverend Stewart came out on the porch, saw the coffin and his initials carved in the lid, he was livid, but contained his anger. The two men quietly took the coffin, put it in a storage shed, telling only those who helped in the mission to search out and destroy stills. The next week, Stewart retaliated by increasing the raids.

By mid-November, word went around about a flogging. The vigilante way of thinking spread like a brush fire out of control. "Meet at the cotton gin north of Draketown tonight. We've got to make plans."

Several men met at the appointed place. Hicksley spoke to the crowd, "Boys we've got to do something. We've got to stop that preacher from Draketown. He and his church members are ruining us. James, Owen, and Hubert Hendrix are willing, Pete and Clyde Barber could be counted on."

Clyde interrupted, "I'll drive and carry men up to Stewart's but I will not be a part to any flogging." A night and time was decided. It was set for just five days after the coffin had been placed on the preacher's porch. Word was passed around.

The appointed Thursday night, November 13, was cold with a wind blowing from the west and a harvest moon shining overhead on those who met at the cotton gin north of Draketown. The Hendrix man and his boys showed up. George Hudson, Tate Gather, Joe Cash and Everett Holder was there. Stan Hester, a sixteen-year-kid, came in drunk. Pete and Tom Barber came in late. All were huddled around smoking and drinking, fuming and planning.

Pete explained as he neared the group, "There's so much smoke rising from you varmints, it looks like the steam rising from the Tallapoosa River on a cold morning." Pete guffawed at his own remark, but no one else appreciated his humor and few even noticed that he had come in, much less heard what he said.

Pete asked, "Where's my cousin, Clyde?" No one answered; only a few looked around.

At 8:00 a late-model black sedan pulled up, carrying eight men inside. The driver, Harry Hicksley, wore a dark wide-brimmed hat. They did not get out of their car and none of those inside spoke, but sat tensely waiting. None of the Draketown boys recognized any of the other men in the sedan. Hicksley signaled it was time and turned toward Draketown.

A second car, an open tonnean, the kind with a soft top that could be lowered on a warmer day, pulled in line behind the sedan. The rest of the men piled into an older-model sedan which followed the other two cars slowly toward Draketown.

On Thursday night, Clyde took Merilou and Ben home early, about 6:00; he had a commitment, a promise to fulfill. When he got to Tamammy's house and dropped off her and her baby, Merilou screamed and ran back to the porch calling after him as he was turning around in the yard to head back.

Tonnean automobile

He parked the truck and went into Tamammy's house and found her laying on the floor. He lifted her onto the bed. Merilou propped her up on a pillow and brought a wet cloth to wipe her face.

"Should I go for Dr. Eaves?" Clyde asked as he looked at Tamammy, seeing her shallow breathing and listless body.

"It's her heart. She's old. Eaves told us last year that she might have a year left. She's lived that last year and now, it's her time."

Merilou ran next door and quickly let other members of Tamammy's family know she was near death. Clyde thought of what he had planned to do; what he had promised—the use of his truck. They'd have to find another vehicle.

He stayed with Merilou and Tamammy and members of their family for several hours. Tamammy looked as though she were in a peaceful sleep. Suddenly, there was a radiance and a smile. They both realized she was gone.

Merilou sobbed for a bit, wiped her eyes and face, and proclaimed, "She was a great lady. She lived through some history that I pray no other generations will ever see."

Merilou suddenly looked at Clyde almost as if she had forgotten he was there. "She was a slave, you know."

"Yes. I know that very well. She and her mother were slaves belonging to my Grandfather "Pap" Barber during the war. They chose to stay with him after the war. They took care of him when he was crippled. I consider Tamammy part of my family. That's why I'm here, now."

Merilou had a far-away look in her eyes and gave Clyde a slight nod. Clyde realized that Merilou had already known what he had just told, but she wanted it said, she wanted it acknowledged as Tamammy slipped from this earth to her heavenly home.

Clyde knew it was time to leave. "I'll go back, and tomorrow I will make arrangements for her funeral. Merilou looked as if she were going to speak, but Clyde held up his hand and said, "I'll take care of it and let you know tomorrow."

By the time Clyde left Tamammy's house and headed home, the night was cold, the wind blew, and the harvest moon had risen high in the clouds that could be seen in the blue-velvet sky.

"You know, cotton used to be king around here, but now corn whisky is king. That's our cash crop."

Chapter 5
Spirits Collide

December 1988

At the beauty shop in Villa Rica each Friday morning right before lunch, a crowd gathered. Some got their hair done, others just came by to hear the stories Arreda told.

About 12:30, the cafe was unusually full, when their patrons gathered around to hear this older silver-haired woman reminisce about the past. Many thought these stories were tall tales and yarns, but Audie Carroll and Arreda and a few other older ones insisted "Oh, this happened. The whole countryside was talking about it. It was in all the newspapers."

On Sundays, preaching about the Holy Spirit resounded from every meetinghouse in every church around the courtyside. Every day of the week, including Sunday, the spirits of alcohol emitted from large seamless kettles to distill in the coils of stills dotted over the countryside. These two spirits were destined to meet, in fact, to collide.

Thursday, November 13, 1924

Three car loads of men drove slowly and quietly up Cotton Gin Road and turned right to the Draketown Main Road—the dirt road through Draketown. The first car parked in front of John Reeves' Mercantile store. With the lights on and the motors running, one man dressed in dark clothing got out of the lead car and without fully closing the car door, walked quickly to Reeves' Store next door to the parsonage.

The owner of the grocery, John Reeves, who had taken the gas lamp from the shelf and was preparing to extinguishing it, jerked his head around in surprise when this stranger walked into his establishment so late at night—just before closing time. "Where's the parsonage?"

John stepped out the door and pointed, "It's just around the corner there —next door."

"We're going on a liquor raid," the tall stranger said in an authoritative voice. "We want you to go wake the parson to go with us."

Mrs. Reeves came out the front door of the store, looking apprehensively at the man who wore a dark, wide-brimmed hat.

John R. Reeves, Sr., Courtesy Judy Hoffman

Reeves, giving his wife a nervous glance, turned left toward the parsonage. He walked swiftly toward Reverend Robert Stewart's two-story parsonage. His step faltered for an instant when he saw the three T-Model automobiles parked in a line along side him as he walked to the parson's house. He could tell in the dark that there were several men in each of these cars.

Reeves mounted the porch steps and rapped sharply and loudly on the plain wooden door. He heard some rustling around as he peered at the dark windows, realizing the pastor had already retired for the night.

Alice was the first to hear the knocking; she woke the pastor. "You're wanted at the door."

In a minute or so, a faint glow came from the window and soon a sleepy Reverend Stewart opened the door. He held a gas lamp at arm's distance and peered into the dark.

Pearl King Reeves, Courtesy Judy Hoffman

"Whose out there?" he demanded.

"It's me," Reeves replied. "There's some men here wanting you to go with them on a raid."

Stewart, who had stepped out onto the porch with his lamp, looked into the night seeing the shapes of three black cars with their bright lights shining into the cold November night. A gust of wind blew the sycamore leaves from a nearby tree onto the ground and at the same time blew against Stewart who wore only a thin night shirt and a toboggan brought down on his head. Stewart felt a surge of impatience; then, excitement and a tinge of fear.

"I'll be dressed and back out as soon as I can." He hurried in to dress quickly, so as not to leave them waiting too long.

After Stewart went back inside, the line of three vehicles pulled up so that the second car was even with the front door of the parsonage. These cars parked, across the road, just off the right side of the road in an open area.

When Stewart had pulled on pants, shirt, a coat and warm hat, he sat on the edge of the bed to put on his socks and shoes.

Alice, still awake, asked, "Why are you getting dressed? Where are you going?"

As he left the room without a word, she was up and followed the lamp light as it went to the front room where her husband left the lamp on a table in front of the window.

Alice, in her long night gown, stood at the window and watched her husband quickly cross the porch, descend the two front steps, and head across the yard. As she took in the scene, her heart begin to pound as she saw the three vehicles. In an instant, she had a vision of the coffin on the porch with her husband's initials carved on it. She opened the door and stood barefoot in the doorway, watching Robert. She saw him hesitate and look back toward her. Alice looked to the right—down to the store; she could make out the silhouette of both John and Pearl Reeves standing in the doorway of their store which was lit by the light of the lamp inside.

"What can I do for you gentlemen?" Her husband's commanding voice cut through the icy chill of the night. The tall man wearing a wide-brimmed hat met him in the yard beside the roadway.

"Preacher. Come with us. We're heading to a liquor still. We're taking it out."

Robert naturally curious, stepped to the middle, nearest car to see if he knew any of the men. As he drew near the center car, he recognized some of the men and immediately became suspicious. He paused, remembering he had neglected to get his pistol. He started to turn back and was seized from behind and pushed toward the car.

"Damn you—you've made your last raid!" someone shouted angrily. Several men grabbed him and shoved him bodily into the second open car—the tonnean, where he was pinned down by its occupants. Stewart, a small man, was overtaken by two men who tried to gag him and bind his wrists and ankles. When one man shoved a gag into his mouth, he tied it tightly behind Stewart's head. Before the gag went into his mouth he hollered out "No! Stop!" The muffled screams were heard by John and Pearl Reeves. Another man grabbed Stewart's wrists and tried to wrap a cord around them. But Stewart was swinging with both fists. The other man, was reaching for his ankles, but Stewart was kicking for all he was worth.

John Reeves stepped back into his store, grabbed his shotgun and started out the door again to assist the pastor when Mrs. Reeves grabbed her husband by the arm, saying "They may have guns. If you go out there, you'll be killed!"

"Get out of the way, I'm going to help the preacher." He made a motion to go out the door and she stepped in front of him, blocking him, "Over my dead body you will." She seized him and prevented him from leaving the store.

Alice, who had come out on the porch, saw what had happened and heard her husband call out. She ran back inside the house, and in a matter of seconds, was running across the yard toward the cars. She was holding Robert's pistol.

Still in her night clothes and barefoot, she cried out to the men to let her husband go as she ran into the midst of the gang. "Please release him! Don't hurt him! Let him go!"

Her heart was beating so fast, she went weak with fear. She knew these men were up to no good. She just did not have time to think, but reacted.

She could see their silhouettes in the moonlight and could almost make out some of the faces of those peering from the vehicles and of those who were struggling with her husband inside the car. The two men who had put her husband into the car, turned toward her.

"Please let him go!" She begged.

They took several steps toward her. She brought the pistol up and fired twice in quick succession, aiming low to strike the men in their knees. One man staggered and fell. Another groped at the side of the car and lunged inside. Alice was still pointing the gun toward the men when their little daughter, Lorene, appeared on the porch of the parsonage and screamed, "Mama!"

Alice, distracted, turned her head and called out, "Lorene, go back inside."

Robert heard a third shot at close range. The deafening roar sent pain through his eardrums. One of the men who had bound Robert's hands in front of him and who now held Robert down so his ankles could be bound was surprised and relaxed his hold. The man whom Alice shot fell into the car, creating a distraction. Robert struggled, kicking off the bindings around his ankles, and pulled away to exit the car from the other side.

This close-range shot came from just outside the rear, third, car. Alice was hit in the right arm, just above the elbow. The force of the bullet spun her around and plunged her forward facedown on the ground.

As Alice lay prostrate, Robert saw a man from the rear automobile fire another shot into her body. In the excitement, Robert managed to escape. After he sprang from the car, he ran across the street toward Dr. Hogue's house for help. The doctor was coming out his front door. Stewart turned toward Alice who lay on the ground.

The would-be abductors panicked. One of them stooped down and picked her up. He threw her body to the side of the road to make room for the three vehicles to flee.

When Robert reached Alice, he saw the automobiles get under way. When he reached where his wife lay, he knelt and even though he still had his wrists bound, he picked up the pistol she still held, clutched in her hand, and fired two shots toward the speeding cars, which were now 50 yards away. Two shots were fired back at him from the cars, as they disappeared into the darkness.

When the commotion had started, the store owner, Reeves, had tried to run out and stop what was happening when his wife had grabbed him. Now both John and Pearl Reeves were at the pastor's side.

Several people ran to the injured Alice lying, unconscious, face down on the ground. Robert was the first to reach her. He was sobbing and repeating his wife's name. Doctor W. L. Hogue, who lived immediately across the street from the parsonage, was beside him, fully dressed, with a lantern in one hand and his doctor's bag in the other. He heard the series of shots and knew something terrible had happened. This was a tight-knit, small Christian community. To hear shots in the night was the same as hearing an alarm blast. Jesse Hogue ran from their house to Lorene who was crying on the porch after watching what had happened to her mother.

"Call Sheriff Richards!" someone shouted. John Reeves ran back to his store to use the phone to call Sheriff George Richards at Buchanan.

Dr. Hogue, who was at Alice's side seconds after the cars sped out of sight, removed the bindings on the pastor's wrists. Robert carefully scooped up his wife to carry her inside.

Jesse Hogue took Lorene inside to her room and wrapped her in a blanket. She was crying hysterically and shaking uncontrollably from the cold and the fear of the scene she had witnessed.

Pearl Reeves came into the parsonage to assist Jesse in caring for Lorene. They met Tannie on the stairway coming out of her bedroom rubbing the sleep from her eyes with the back of her fist.

"I was standing at the window and saw what happened. I even saw the man who shot my mother," Tannie told them as tears filled her eyes. She slipped on the robe she carried and made her way down the stairs as Robert brought her mother into the house; she lay limp in his arms. Blood covered her long night gown.

All attention turned to the wounded Alice. Robert laid her on their bed as Dr. Hogue brought the kerosene lamp from the front room. Robert went to get wet cloths and a pitcher of water to fill the basin to wash away the blood. Dr. Hogue began to assess the injuries from the gunshots. There was one wound on her right arm and there was blood all down her back. The mattress under Alice was soon soaked red.

Dr. Eaves, who had an office and a home just down the street, came quickly into the room with his doctor's bag.

Could Alice survive these gunshots? She was a thin, willowy, graceful lady, but she was strong. She usually rose everyday at sun up to do her work for the Lord. She was a model of the blessed woman, serving the Lord as a pastor's wife by ministering charitably to the needs of the community, while at the same time caring for their children and taking care of her household.

Tannie was busy; she carried a wet cloth for Pearl Reeves to wash Lorene's face as she held her in her lap to console her, telling her that her mother would be okay. Tannie went to her mother. Dr. Hogue asked Tannie to bring another lamp and place it on the small table beside the bed so he could assess the wounds. He told Tannie to bring the scissors and then to go sit with his wife and stay with Lorene. As Tannie, whose face was streaked with tears, left the room, she looked back at her mother laying pale and lifeless on the bed.

Alice was unconscious. Hogue lifted the right side of her body so as to view her back. Dr. Eaves came around to that side of the bed to observe the wounds. With the scissors, he carefully cut the nightgown away to reveal the mortal wound on her spine in the middle of her back. The man who fired the last bullet, shot into her back as she lay face down.

Dr. Hogue gently relaxed his hold and allowed Alice to lie flat on the bed. He tilted his hat back to rub his forehead as he looked at both Eaves and Robert who had waited wordlessly. "I can't help her. We've got to get her to Atlanta. And soon."

"I'll bring my car around and take her to Atlanta. That's all we can do," Dr. Eaves told Robert. He left to walk back home to get his car.

Jesse Hogue left Lorene upstairs with Tannie and Pearl Reeves to assist her husband in caring for Alice. When she saw Alice lying on the bed in her blood-soaked nightgown, she looked as though she would faint. She began to cry softly, sat in a nearby chair, and prayed rapidly in a quiet voice.

Dr. Hogue attended to Alice; he bandaged both the wound on her arm and the gaping, open wound in her spinal column. Mrs. Jesse Hogue had, with the doctor's help, changed her nightgown and wrapped her in blankets getting her ready for the trip to Atlanta.

There was noise in the front room. Reverend Stewart and Dr. Hogue looked up when Sheriff Richards came into the bedroom. He was red-faced, even on this cold night, but his face was red because of anger.

Dr. Hogue denounced, "This was a gang of rum-runners and they were out to flog Reverend Stewart—to give him a horse whipping."

Sheriff Richards' presence filled the room. He was a big man—tall, big-boned, and muscular. He stood quietly and studied Alice lying so gravely near death on the bed. He took his hat off and held it, turning the brim little by little as he studied her solemnly—almost reverently for what seemed like minutes. He looked at Dr. Hogue who was taking Alice's blood pressure and nodded toward Mrs. Hogue who was putting another blanket on Alice. All were quiet as he assessed the situation. Sheriff Richards sighed, made eye contact with Robert, and motioned toward the door. They both left the room quietly.

When Stewart and the Sheriff got to the front room, Stewart said, "I recognized six of the men. All moonshiners who have been constant trouble-makers."

"It was James Hendrix and his two sons, Owen and Hubert, and Tate Gather, and Pete Barber. It was Stan Hester—the first man I saw of the gang—who fired one of the shots that hit my wife. They took off, north. We've got to go after them," the reverend informed in his broadest "preacher voice."

"I'll rouse a posse of men and meet back here as soon as I can, hopefully within the hour," Sheriff Richards stated emphatically. With the information Stewart had given him, Sheriff Richards hurriedly left to round up men and go after the attackers.

Upstairs, Pearl Reeves put the daughters back to bed and sat with them the rest of the night.

About a half hour later, Dr. Eaves brought his car around to the parsonage to take Alice into Atlanta. Together, Reverend Stewart and Dr. Hogue placed the mortally wounded Alice on the back seat of Dr. Eaves car. Reverend Stewart rode in the back with her as Dr. Eaves drove the two-hour trip from Draketown. They arrived at Wesley Memorial Hospital about 1:00 a.m.

Doctor Eaves never left Alice's side while the physicians at Wesley Memorial Hospital fought to save her life. One bullet penetrated her elbow and the second shot had entered near her spine and turned upward, shattering several vertebrae. When Alice regained consciousness, it was evident she was paralysed; she could barely move her head.

After Reverend Stewart admitted Alice to the hospital, he drove Doc Eaves' car back to Draketown to join the posse. He wanted vengeance. He wanted justice. The more moonshiners he put behind bars, the better things would be.

At the parsonage, after Alice was taken to the hospital, men began to gather in the yard. Dr. Hogue, his wife, Jesse, and John and Pearl Reeves stayed inside to answer the phone and make coffee for those who came on such a cold night.

When Jackson Bingham learned that Alice Stewart had been shot, he was in a state of numb disbelief. He dreaded the sorrow those two daughters would feel if she did not survive. He dreaded telling his family, especially Arreda. She would be devastated for her two young friends. He was among those of the community who had heard the shots and who had come immediately to help. He had gone back inside his house to roust his sons, Boots and Bud. They were old enough to help search. He sent them to knock on doors and get others to join the posse.

Life is about the choices you make; sometimes these choices can be influenced by desperation: The preacher chose to fight alcohol; the moonshiners chose to make shine; those who made the poor choice to be part of the attack that night, should have been held accountable.

Chapter 6
Two Night Riders Wounded

After the attack on the parson and his wife, the three moonshiner's vehicles sped out of town going west then turned right going north toward Buchanan-Dallas Road. When they were in a clearing, the lead car pulled over. Several men got out of each car.

The tall man in the wide-brimmed black hat, Hicksley, stepped from the first car and went rapidly to the rear car and jerked the door open then he saw a gaping hole between the front and back windows. He shouted, "Are you crazy! You shot the pastor's wife. Twice!" He grabbed the youngest of the group by the neck.

"We weren't going there to kill anybody. We were just going to teach the pastor a lesson to leave us alone and quit destroying our stills. Sure we're all angry. But this got out of hand."

He grasp the sixteen-year-old kid by the neck, choking him. He was angry and the kid was struggling to breathe.

James Hendrix, one of the older moonshiners, growled, "Let him go. "It's done now, and we can't undo it."

Hicksley angrily spun around to face Hendrix, "Where'd he get that pistol anyway? We weren't supposed to bring guns to this shindig. He's underage. That's not his gun, someone gave it to him! What are you all thinking? Why did he have it?"

"I didn't know he brought it," replied one of the men, lamely.

Another man added, "When the pastor's wife shot at us, she hit Burk in the knee and Hubert in the side of the leg."

Hicksley peered inside and on the seat was Burk with his coat wrapped around his knee, and even in the moonlight, Hicksley could make out the dark wetness all over the seat. Burk began to groan as if on cue.

"Well she got what she deserved—shooting us like that," said Hubert who was holding his leg, in awful pain. Hubert was pale and looked as though he might keel over any second.

"You idiot! She didn't deserve to be shot; she was defending her husband. She's a pastor's wife. You don't shoot women! Especially her. She's a nice lady. You yellow-livered coward!"

Hicksley pulled the door open further to enter when Hubert stopped him by saying, "We got other problems. Barber here has been shot. See where this car's been shot."

The panel between the front and back windows was gone; there was a gaping hole instead. The driver of the third car was Tom Barber. Upon examining him, Hicksley determined that he had not been shot. Glass from the exploded car window was all over his back. In trying to talk to Tom, he decided that his hearing had been temporarily affected. Tom sat very still, not moving a muscle, facing forward as though he was in shock. But he had managed to drive this far.

It seemed as the three vehicles had driven from the scene, the parson had grabbed the gun his wife still had in her hand and fired at the cars, hitting the last one behind the front window, knocking out most of it.

"Tom Barber. Are you okay?" Tom nodded, but did not speak.

"He's just stunned; he will probably be okay after a while," the short, thin man stated. "We've got to get these two wounded men to the doctor."

"Well this is a fine kettle of fish. Two wounded and the pastor's wife shot."

"Any ideas?" Hendrix asked. He looked at the men. Many were shaking from the cold, from the excitement created at the scene, but most were high on their own likker. How else would they have had the nerve to go confront the pastor, a well-respected powerful man in this part of Georgia.

"We can't just stand here." After a quick discussion by the one or two who were sober, they decided to split up—three ways of course. Each vehicle was to be driven with the lights off as long as the driver could see by moonlight. The roads were dirt made up partly of sand which showed up light enough to keep them in the road.

Second Car

The two wounded men, Burke and Hubert Hendrix, were moved to the second car, the tonnean. Tom Barber, in shock and suffering a hearing loss, would be taken home. The second car was driven to Cleburne County, Alabama, just ten miles over the line about fifty miles from Draketown. They had friends there. Someone could pay the doctor off—to patch them up and to keep quiet about who he treated. No names would be given, anyway.

"Don't come back to Draketown limping. That would be like throwing up a red flag," Hicksley told them.

The two moonshiners with leg wounds stayed in Alabama with friends until their wounds healed and they walked without limping.

The Damaged Third Car

Pete Barber took the shot-up vehicle north to Yorkville to dispose of it. There were plenty of old copper mines up Yorkville Road beyond the town. After half an hour driving on a dirt road with the lights cut, Pete slowly approached an old mine; he could just make out a silhouette of a framed board shack where the watchman stayed near the entrance. As he approached, he flipped on the headlights and the night watchman came out carrying a flashlight and a shotgun.

"Who's out there? What you want?" He shined the light on the single driver and recognized him. "Pete Barber, what are you doing up here this time of night?" Then the light from his flashlight hit on the gaping hole in the side of the car.

"Well!" He spoke emphatically then his tone became one of teasing, "What do we have here? This time of night and this situation—someone has been up to something illegal!" That put the night watchman at an advantage. He knew he was going to be asked to do something.

"There's been an incident. I need to get rid of this car," he explained.

The night watchman went around to the passenger side, got in and said, "I'll have to do a little thinking on that."

He got into the car because it was cold, because he did not want to be seen if anyone else came up, and because he had to decide not just where to put something as large as a car—he knew immediately the answer to that, but he had to spend a few minutes thinking mainly how much he was going to ask in exchange for this favor. Pete cut the lights of the car and they sat in the dark outside the mining shack.

"First, I need to know what I'm getting involved in. Did anybody get killed?"

"No nothing like that. We were trying to take the preacher out and horsewhip him to make him leave us and our stills alone; he shot at us to scare us away. Nobody got killed. He just fired at us as we drove away."

"Alright. I think I know an abandoned mine—no copper has come out of there in fifty years and the mining company is not apt to look in there ever again. Now if I get caught hiding this car, I could go to jail. I need $50 to hide this car and a gallon of moonshine every week until Christmas to make sure I keep quiet."

Pete, nervous, cold, scared, and hung over, had become desperate and would have agreed to almost anything, "I don't have $50 on me. But I can bring it in a few days. As to the moonshine, no problem."

"I need you to bring the $50 by one week from now—next Friday morning."

"Okay. Okay. Let's do something. I can't keep sitting here."

The night watchman went into the shack and came back within a few minutes and got into the damaged vehicle. The lights came on, the motor started, and the car made its way slowly for several miles through a winding road and many hills. This country was the foothills at the edge of the Appalachian Mountains which ended in northwest Georgia. Had it been daylight, the view would have been breathtaking. But at this point, Pete and his passenger gazed through the front window at the lit area pushed forward by the slowly moving car.

"I think this is it. Stop here. Right over there is the entrance." A white painted board with the dark fading letters spelling out: R E E D C O P P E R M I N E.

"This is where the first copper was found in 1854. Yield was good 'til the '70s, I've heard. Been cleared out for fifty years. No one will ever come here. I'm sure of it."

"This is where things get spooky. Drive in."

"Are you crazy! I'm not driving in there. That would be like driving into my own tomb. I'm paying you $50; you drive."

The watchman got out, stood, and thought. It would be better if he did drive in himself. He could not trust this half-sober feller, anyway, to do it right.

"Alright. You stand over there, by that last hill," he indicated about 200 yards back down the road away from the entrance.

"I've got the flashlight, dynamite, and the matches." Pete Barber got out of the car. The half-sober, scared Pete went two-hundred yards back down the way they had come.

The watchman moved some wooden barriers that blocked the entrance and tossed them aside. He got into the vehicle, going ever so slowly over old debris which created a bumpy, almost impossible ride. About one-fourth mile into the shaft, he decided it was not safe to go any further. He got out of the car, placed the dynamite into the gas tank, struck the match to it, and ran like hell toward the entrance.

His only light was the flashlight he carried aimed at the rocky path he had just driven over. One-fourth mile. He wondered as he ran, 'was the fuse of the dynamite long enough for him to make it that far before the dynamite blew?' If he had time he would have had second thoughts about that $50 dollars. He knew he was close to the entrance when he could breathe in fresh, cold night air.

Thank heavens he could see the stars above, but he did not slow down. He could make out Pete's silhouette in the dark and headed toward him. Just as he reached this half-sober feller, the explosion shook the earth. The percussion boom rattled his eardrums. Both guys fell to the ground. Either the percussion knocked them down or they fell to the ground as a reflex actions.

Pete was the first to recover. "That could have been heard for miles around."

"Yeah it could." But who is within those miles to hear it?" He gave a little chuckle.

"How we gonna get back?"

The watchman chuckled again, "We gonna walk. It would be a lot better to be back before daylight. Might be better if we hide you in my vehicle after we get there. I'll drop you off in Draketown, come morning."

The First Car

The other men, close to fifteen, either walked home or rode in the first car—the late model sedan; some stood on the running board and held on through the windows. Shivering with cold and fright, the drunken moonshiners riding in the sedan reflected on what had just happened.

"We're going to have to lay low for a while until this blows over."

Another one said, "This storm is not going to blow over anytime soon. If this lady dies, somebody will burn in the electric chair—somebody will ride 'Old Sparky' for this."

They were dropped off near their house to walk quietly and avoid the road. If a vehicle came by, they were to lie in the bushes away from the roadside until it was safe to make their way home and go to bed. Some were sober at least in mood by the cold, by the physical exertion, but mainly from the realization of what they had done. By this time, the last of those in the third car were home; it was about 1:00 a.m. Friday morning.

Rumor was that the car with the bullet holes was taken to Yorkville, driven into one of the abandoned gold mines or copper mines and covered up—buried. No one ever saw the automobile again.

Chapter 7
The Posse

December 1988

When Arreda told Trisha and the ladies at the beauty shop and the crowd at the cafe what happened to Alice Stewart, they were shocked.

"This all happened after I had gone to bed. I heard the booms, but thought it was thunder and went back to sleep. My bedroom is on that corner of the house and I could have gone to the window and saw it all happen. But my daddy told us the next morning at breakfast after he came in from the all night search with the posse. I was devastated to hear that Tannie and Lorene's mother had been shot and that anyone would want to hurt her. I thought of Tannie and Lorene and wanted to be with them."

After 11:00 p.m., Sheriff Richards left the little parsonage to awaken the men of the neighborhood, form a posse, and search for the assailants who attacked the parson and Alice Stewart. He aroused more than two-score men, incensed residents of the county and surrounding sections, to gather in front of the Stewart's home. He swore them in and prepared them to scour the surrounding woods and hills.

Reverend Stewart had a wide following in this part of the country. Many members of his congregation were among the sheriff's posse who sought to capture his would-be abductors. Stewart called his assistant, Guy Austin, and soon the front yard was filled with the men of his congregation who were in great sorrow to hear of Alice's serious wounds.

The deacons came quietly into the house without speaking to anyone, went to the pastor's study, and knelt down in prayer. These six men each prayed for Alice, for her recovery, and that they gather enough posse to hunt safely without anyone else getting hurt. Several prayed fervently, wiping their eyes with their handkerchief as they stood. These sorrow-struck church members were determined to find the culprits. Soon there were enough men in front of the parson's house that Sheriff Richards divided them into two groups.

One group of men took up the trail of one of the cars, which led into Alabama then the trail was lost. This part of the posse returned disheartened to the parsonage.

One of the cars was tracked as far as Lindale, northwest of Yorkville, where the trail was lost. As they tracked that particular car, they noticed an impression in the dirt road created by a nub in the tire. By going slowly with the headlights on this trail, they were able to follow the nub imprint toward the old copper mine area. But here other tracks made by the miners going to work the day before blurred the nubbed tire imprint. The trail was lost in this area and they could not pick it up again.

The other half of the posse scoured the thickly wooded territory for miles. About 1:00 a.m., the other party of searchers passing the house of Tate Gather near Draketown heard a door slam. They stopped and found Gather in bed, but fully clothed. He was taken into custody and jailed at the county seat of Buchanan, Haralson County.

The Bingham Family on Friday Morning

Some posse members left their search to return home for breakfast, a few hours of sleep; then, would return to join the others. Jackson, Boots, and Bud were back home at 8:00.

Each member of the household was awake and each knew something serious had happened, but Melviney told them, "Jackson will tell you when he gets home."

When Jackson heard the shots the night before, he had quickly drew on a robe and shoes and went to the parsonage to see Alice carried in. He had talked to Mrs. Reeves before she went into the parsonage. Pearl had told him what had happened, having witnessed what occurred.

Jackson had gone back to his bedroom and told Melviney, "Alice Stewart has been shot by a gang of the preacher's enemies; I'm getting our boys and we're going to see what we can do to help. Don't tell the twins or Arreda. I will do that in the morning—or when I get back to the house."

About 8:00 the next morning, when Jackson, Boots, and Bud walked into the kitchen, Melviney, Arreda, Alpha and Omega, looked up. Boots and Bud did not make eye contact with any of them, but each pulled out a chair and sat at the kitchen table without a word.

Jackson sat down, looked at each one. "A tragedy happened last night."

He motioned for Arreda who went to him; he pulled her into his lap and continued.

"Some men came by the parsonage and had a confrontation. Alice Stewart was shot. Twice. She was taken to the hospital in Atlanta."

Arreda began to cry and buried her head into her daddy's shoulders. Alpha and Omega were speechless. Omega covered her mouth and sat staring, unseeing, at the kitchen table. Alpha got up and began cooking scrambled eggs for the family. Tears streamed down her face, which she wiped away with the back of her hand and wiped the back of her hand on her long cotton dress.

Bud declared, "We'll get the ones who did this. There's about forty men. The sheriff split them into two groups—twenty men in each posse. Some went all the way to Alabama; some followed a trail to Yorkville. We've come to get some sleep then we're going back out."

Melviney studied the family and kept thinking, 'What could we do?'

Boots had the answer. "Poor Tannie and the little girl. I feel sorry for them. What if . . ."

Melviney intervened by putting her hand on his shoulder, making eye contact and shaking her head.

As she stood to get a pan of hot biscuits out of the oven, she said, "I will go right over and have the daughters come stay with us. They must be devastated."

The family seemed to send silent thoughts of approval: Arreda and Boots looked at her, nodding. Jackson nodded to her and began to serve his plate. Melviney left without eating.

She grabbed her coat and was at the parsonage in minutes. Several cars were outside and a stranger answered the door. The front room was packed with people she did not know.

"I live next door and would like to see the girls," she told someone.

"Well, they're too upset for company," this person said, rejecting her request.

Tannie came downstairs. "It's okay. Mrs. Bingham can come upstairs with me."

Melviney realized she would have to be aggressive.

"Tannie, you and Lorene need to come home with me. We have breakfast ready and Boots and Arreda want to see you."

She followed Tannie up the stairway. Tannie paused and looked back down into the living room and realized they would be better off at Melviney's house. After all, the Binghams were like family; they had lived next door to them for a year now.

When they got to Lorene's room, she was lying on the bed awake. Pearl Reeves was still with her; she had slept in a big chair beside the bed last night.

"Is my mother dead?"

"No Honey. We will pray that the Lord will help her recover." Mrs. Reeves told her.

When Arreda saw Melviney, she threw back the covers, jumped out of bed, ran to her, and threw her arms around her. "Did you hear what happened to my mother?"

Melviney hugged her, went to the bed, sat down, and drew her onto her lap. She held her for a long time, after saying, "How would you and Tannie like to come have breakfast with us?"

Lorene nodded vigorously. Tannie was already laying out Lorene's clothes and shoes and getting their coats.

Clyde Barber on Friday Morning

The Friday morning after the attack at the parsonage, Clyde Barber was up early to take care of the funeral arrangements for Tamammy Hart. He drove his truck to Draketown with the intention of buying a coffin at Oss Carroll's store. When he got into town, something was very different. Small crowds of people gathered together in little clusters, talking. When he got to the parsonage, people stood on the porch and in the yard. The sheriff's car was parked out front. He saw Jackson Bingham walking toward his home with his two sons.

He pulled over, let the window down, and asked, "Is there something going on?"

Bingham slowed down to answer and his two sons waited to hear what their dad told him. All three of them looked tired, like they had not slept. All looked tense.

Bingham told Barber, "A gang of men attacked the pastor last night. It was probably the ones he tore up their stills. They got him into a car and were gagging and tying him when his wife came out and fired at them. They fired at her and she was shot twice. One of those times, she was shot while she lay face down on the ground.

She's in the hospital in Atlanta. It doesn't look good. About forty men have been out all night looking for those in the gang."

Barber went pale and managed to mumble, "Sorry to hear that," nodded and slowly drove his truck to Carroll's store.

He parked at the store and sat there stunned. He had to collect himself before he talked to anyone. His thoughts raced, 'what if I had been with them? They were supposed to give the parson a warning by roughing him up a bit. Nobody was supposed to get shot. The preacher's wife shot?' He had seen her a couple of times and thought her a kind and graceful, attractive lady. She showed that she really cared when he saw her at Naomi's funeral. He could not imagine her being shot in the back as she lay face down on the ground or her lying in a hospital bed in Atlanta.

His thoughts turned to his cousins. 'I'll bet the posse are after Pete and Tom. They may be on the run and come to my house.' He tried to put that aside in his mind for a while. He bucked up and went into the store, bought a coffin for Tamammy, and pulled around back to load it. People in the store were talking about what had happened. Several ladies were crying and remembering Alice Stewart like she had already died.

Clyde walked over to Eaves' office. No one answered the door. He walked behind the office to the house and knocked. Mrs. Eaves slowly opened the door and peaked out, looking apprehensive. She looked relieved to see it was Clyde and opened the door and invited him to come in from the cold.

"I just stopped by to tell Dr. Eaves that Tamammy Hart died last night. Thought he would want to know."

"Well, I'm sorry to hear about her passing. She was a good woman and lived a long time. That's like a legend passing," Mrs. Nettie Eaves paused and looked thoughtful, remembering Tamammy.

"I will tell my husband about her passing when he calls," she said. "He's in Atlanta with Alice Stewart. I guess you've heard about what happened last night. Ben—my husband, was up, dressed and out the door in minutes when he heard the shooting. He told me later there were three cars loaded down with men; they had left heading north right before he reached Alice. Dr. Hogue was the first at her side before anyone. But there wasn't anything either of them could do. They shot her in the arm and in the back. He vowed not to leave her side."

Clyde was getting a knot in his stomach, picturing the shooting of this innocent woman. "Well, I'll go. Hope everything turns out well for her," he stammered and left.

Clyde headed down toward Tamammy's to deliver the coffin. As he drove near the Phillip's farm, he was surprised to see Pete walking out of the woods toward him. He had been waiting for Clyde to go after Merilou like he did every morning. He opened the door of the truck and got in. "You heard what happened?"

Clyde grabbed him by the shirt at the neck, punched him in the face and then the stomach. "You G__ D___ Idiot. You ought to have been shot—not Alice Stewart."

Pete took the punches and verbal abuse like he expected it. "Calm down. Calm down." he hollered. "You've got to take us away from this county. It's crawling with deputies. There's men everywhere looking for us."

Clyde looked up to see Tom run out of the woods toward the truck.

Clyde felt alarm. He had to get away from them. He had to get rid of them. He did not want to be seen with these moonshiner cousins. Just being kin to them was implication enough and there the three of them were in broad daylight.

Pete filled him in. "The car Tom was driving was shot. Glass went all over his shoulders and his hearing has been affected, but I think he will be alright, in time. We both went home, but decided it was not safe to stay there. We really need to get out of sight."

Clyde thought fast. "Okay. One of you get into the coffin. The other get under the truck bed."

Tom looked at him in questioning.

Clyde explained quickly, "That where I put my haul—under the truckbed. Don't worry, it's large enough for you."

He showed Tom where the crawl space was under the truck bed. Tom crawled in; then, Pete and Clyde jumped up onto the back of the truck. Pete got into the coffin; Clyde secured the lid. He had already secured the coffin with a rope onto the back of the truck when he bought it.

Clyde worried about this situation as he drove. 'What if he were pulled over?'

Just before the turn off to Tamammy's, members of the posse came down the road toward him. When they neared him, they motioned for him to pull over.

"Clyde Barber, what you doing out this early? What you got in the back there," one of them demanded.

Clyde came back at them, "One of the negros down at Mud Creek Road died last night. I'm delivering the coffin." One of the men got out of the vehicle and walked around to the back.

Clyde added, "Just bought it at Carroll's store; got to get it delivered in time for the funeral this morning. I'm in a hurry." Clyde had broken out into a cold sweat, even thought it was a chilly November day.

With that the man seemed satisfied. He got back into the car loaded with members of the posse, most of which carried a shotgun. As they sped off, several turned to look at the coffin on the back of the truck.

Clyde turned down Tamammy's road, continued past her house, and went about eight miles north. When he stopped, he went around back and demanded Pete and Tom get out. "This is cutting it close. I'm due to carry this coffin in time for the funeral. What if the posse goes to Tamammy's to check and see if I'm there?"

Pete climbed out. "Never thought I'd have to get into a coffin before I'm dead!" he guffawed like he had said the funniest thing in the world. The other two gave him a hard look.

Clyde left Pete and Tom in the woods and hightailed it back to Tamammy's. It had taken him half an hour to go the eight miles north and back.

When he got to her house, he spoke to those around and unloaded the coffin. He told Merilou that he could not stay for the funeral; he had some pressing business. She nodded and thanked him, assuring him that they could handle the funeral arrangements.

"Telma fed Junior a bottle this morning," he told Merilou. "After the funeral, I'll come and get you about twelve."

Merilou agreed. Clyde left to get back to the farmhouse. He was shaken and hoped he did not see or hear of his cousins anytime soon.

Toby and Mollie Howard on Friday Morning

Toby had heard his Hendrix uncle and cousins planning on getting even with Pastor Stewart, but he told them right up front that he wanted no part of any violence.

"I don't care how many times he tears up our stills, we can always rebuild in a different place. We done it three times this year already. It's a lot of work, but it keeps us from getting caught. There are creeks all around this part of the country. Some run north to south, some come off the Tallapoosa River, and one curves around like a horse shoe sitting on its side, east to west. All these creeks are in the deep woods. We can keep moving; we've always done that. You three do what you feel you have to do, but leave me out of it. I'm not going to hurt anybody."

On Thursday night, no one showed up to man the still. Just him. This was the third day—when the liquor was ready to pour into containers. He kept the fire going. That was fine with him as it was unusually cold with a wind blowing. He sat and added logs to the fire all night. After midnight, he realized they should have returned by then.

He thought to himself, 'How long does it take a bunch of men to go beat up a preacher? He's even a small man.' Toby began to worry. What if something had happened?

His attention turned to the job at hand. This was usually a three-man job. He did the best he could. At daybreak, he left the still to cut through the woods, take a back road, and walk home.

He could see enough to get through the thick underbrush. Even though most folks in these parts rose early, they had chores—milking the cows and feeding the animals. He didn't expect to see anyone.

Faintly from far away, he heard a sound coming from behind him that didn't belong in a woods: hound dogs barking and howling. Hound dogs were good for two things: tracking coons at night or tracking a man.

Toby began to run toward home. In the woods ahead, he heard the brakes of a car screeching—metal to metal, coming to a stop. With dogs maybe a mile behind him and a vehicle ahead of him, he cut to the right. He knew a short-cut over a ridge to his house. He ran up the sharp bank of a high hill, risky because a man can be seen on a hill from below—especially one on the move. Better off to lie down, but he would lose time. It would only be a matter of time until the hounds picked up his scent.

Toby ran hard. It was a cold morning and he could see his breath coming in white puffs as he cut his way through the trees and underbrush. Soon he was at the crest of the ridge, but did not dare pause to look back at the winding road below. He was down the other side and to his shack in half an hour.

Toby went into his house; no one was up. He undressed quickly in the kitchen and eased quietly into the bedroom so as not to wake his wife. He slipped under the warm quilts. Mollie roused up to look at him with questions in her eyes.

"Go back to sleep. If anyone comes to the door and asks for me, come to wake me like I've been here all night. Don't ask questions now. Try and go back to sleep."

Ten minutes later, Toby and Mollie heard the sound of a car coming into the yard; then, a sharp knock at the door.

"You go," Toby whispered.

Mollie put on her robe, walked quickly to the door, and opened it as if she had just been awaken. Before she could ask any questions, Sheriff Richards pushed passed her into the kitchen.

"Where's your husband?"

She tried to look surprised. "Well Sheriff, he's asleep."

At that moment, Toby came in wearing only his union suit, which most men wore during the winter months under their clothes. His hair was all pushed up in the back like he had been sleeping all night.

"Sheriff, what can I do for you this cold morning? Has something happened?" Toby turned to Mollie, "Honey start a fire and make some coffee. These men," referring to the two standing in the door, "look like they could use some."

Richards began to interrogate Toby in a commanding voice. "Howard, there was a gang of men who attacked Reverend Stewart up in Draketown last night. The preacher's wife was shot. He identified your kin as being part of that gang. You know anything about this?"

Howard sat down in a kitchen chair, looking stunned, which was easy to do because he was shocked about the shooting of the parson's wife. He motioned for the other men to come in and close the door. Mollie, who was building up a fire, stopped to stare.

She was the first to reply. "You mean Alice Stewart? She was shot? Well, How is she?" Mollie knew she was giving her husband time to collect himself and think before he spoke.

"She's in critical condition in a hospital in Atlanta," one of the deputies told her.

"Howard, where were you last night, and when have you seen your Uncle James?" Richards demanded.

Toby replied slowly, giving himself time the think. "Well, Sheriff Richards, I was right here sleeping. It was too cold to be out doing anything last night. And as to my Uncle . . ." Toby paused to rub his chin to think. "About three weeks ago I went over to his place to get some apple tree saplings to plant in our orchard. That's the last

I saw of him or any of the Hendrix."

Sheriff Richard regarded Toby for a moment, looked at the deputies, and looked around the room.

He took a big sigh. "Well. Boys, let's be on our way."

By this time Mollie had a fire going. Two of the three visitors in the kitchen went over to warm in front of the blaze. Mollie had gone to the bucket of water that sat on the side table, cracking through the ice to pour some water into the coffee pot.

"I can have this coffee ready in about ten minutes, if you men will stay."

Sheriff Richards motioned for his men as he started for the door. "We could use some coffee, but we've been out all night and need to get back to Draketown to see if there have been any arrests."

When the sheriff and his men were back in the car, the sheriff turned to the others and said, "Did you see the pile of clothes and his boots in the corner of the kitchen? His boots had a lot of mud on them—wet mud—not dried mud from yesterday. It looked to me like he had been in a hurry to get undressed. Why didn't he undress in the bedroom and why would Mollie allow him to leave his things piled up like that? The rest of the house was neat and clean. That looks suspicious to me."

One of the deputies spoke up. "They seem too prosperous for the hard times we've all had lately. I know his kids have new clothes. I saw them all walking together to school back in September. I saw Mollie at least twice up at the mercantile stores buying clothes and groceries. Something's not right. Where's he getting the money?"

"We'll have to watch Toby Howard and see if he's up to something," Richards concluded.

As the cars drove away, Mollie turned to look at Toby. She collapsed in the kitchen chair.

"Just as I had thought. Our lives were getting better and this happens. I just want to cry—to scream." Tears were running down her face.

Toby was shocked; he had never seen Mollie cry since they had been married fifteen years ago.

"Oh Mollie, everything is going to be alright. We'll get through this."

Mollie wiped her tears and began preparing breakfast, not knowing what else to say or do. She could hear the kids getting up.

In an hour, all the kids had been fed, dressed, and sent to school. Mollie spent a tense, quiet day as she went about her routine. She worked in the house caring for the two younger children. Toby slept since he had been up all night at the still.

That afternoon, the children came in all talking at once, telling about their day. "Mama, Tannie and Lorene, you know the preacher's kids? They were not at school. The teacher got up and told us their mama was in a hospital. Somebody shot her. There was a gang who tried to beat up the preacher. We all cried. Then the teacher told us to bow our heads and she said a prayer for their mama. We were scared all day. We were afraid to walk home. We don't want to meet that gang."

Mollie tried to reassure them and calm them down, but she had a feeling like a thorn in her stomach that would not go away.

After the children had a snack and went outside to play, her eldest son, Sandy, her fourteen-year-old tow-headed, blue-eyed darling, came back in to talk to her.

"Mama, I heard Daddy come in early this morning. Then I heard the Sheriff and some men come in and ask questions. Did Daddy have anything to do with that shooting last night?" He looked so serious and fearful of what his mother would answer.

"No Honey. Your Daddy was working last night. But he was not in Draketown and he did not have anything to do with that shooting."

Sandy looked so relieved, smiled at her, and was out the door to run around the yard with his brothers and sisters.

Mollie watched her children from the window and thought about the money in the fruit jar buried in the barn. She wished Toby had quit helping at the Hendrix still. She knew last winter when they were on starvation, that he had been forced into helping them so they could have food. But this spring, summer and fall, they had been spending and had plenty. Should that be a crime? He was committing a crime just to give them plenty. Why should he have to choose? Be a criminal and provide for his family, or reform and starve?

Friday Afternoon

A local newspaper reported that one of the men whom authorities suspected of being a member of the gang had refused to talk to a man who came to his house for the purpose of buying a car, which the former had been very anxious to sell. According to the story, the man's wife appeared at the door and told the prospective buyer to come back in a few days, saying that her husband had been out in the car "last night."

"He had some trouble," she said and refused to allow him to look at the automobile, which was usually kept in the car house out back.

The prospective buyer of the car left, but as he did, he looked toward the car house and saw that the doors were closed. This owner of the car, authorities believed, was wounded by Mrs. Stewart when she shot into the gang of men. That car was never seen again.

Men Believed Wounded, The Haralson County Tribune Reported

"Before Mrs. Stewart was struck by a bullet from the revolver of one of the men, she had fired two shots from her husband's pistol at close range. Two men were now believed to have been wounded," the population read.

The sheriff's posse launched a sweeping search for Mrs. Stewart's attackers. After Tate Gather had been taken into custody on a charge of suspicion, and after the publicity about the two wounded men was reported in the newspaper, everyone in Haralson County was on the lookout for any man limping or with a bandage of any kind. All night Thursday until Friday night, the posses divided to cover all parts of Haralson county.

Joe Cash, who lived near Draketown, was arrested on the charge of suspicion on Thursday night shortly after the shooting. He was jailed at Buchanan. At that time, authorities refused to divulge how he was connected with the case.

The most astounding arrest came as a shock to the community. John Reeves, the owner of Reeves' Mercantile Store in Draketown, was arrested. He was taken to Buchanan and jailed.

Reeves kept insisting, "I only went to Reverend Stewart's and got him to the door and told him these men wanted him to go on a liquor raid with them. How was I to know that they were out to get the pastor? When I heard the commotion, I started to run to help him, but my wife was afraid I would be hurt or killed. I was not a part of this gang." Nevertheless, Sheriff Richards jailed him until there could be an inquiry.

Late Friday, Sheriff George Richards visited Alice at Wesley Memorial Hospital in Atlanta. He called her attendants to be witnesses with him as to her testimony. When she regained consciousness, Alice told Dr. Eaves and Sheriff Richards and those in attendance around her that Pete Barber was one of the men she saw in the automobiles. She also told him that the first shot came from the rear of the line of automobiles. She did not see who fired the second shot. She whispered this information weakly to Sheriff Richards as he leaned in close to hear her. He wrote down everything Alice told him, word for word.

Saturday Morning

Newspapers reported, "In the early hours of Saturday morning, Tom and Pete Barber, two young brothers, were arrested near Yorkville, about eight miles north of Draketown. They were taken into custody by deputies to Buchanan, and lodged in the county jail."

After Clyde Barber had taken his cousins, Tom and Pete Barber, eight miles north of Draketown and let them out on Friday morning, they spent the day running to get further away from Draketown. As dusk approached, they needed cover. Pete decided to sleep in a barn. Having no food or water in more than twenty-four hours, they stopped by a farm and helped themselves to the well bucket. No one saw them. They went quietly into the barn and slept in the hay.

Early the next morning, they awoke and stumbled around in the barn, startling the mules. When the farmer came with a lantern to see what was wrong, he discovered two tired, hungry, dirty moonshiners on the run.

This farmer never went out to investigate possible trouble without his shotgun. He pointed the double-barreled 12-gauge at them while his grown son tied them up. In time, they were strapped to the back of a truck and taken to Buchanan.

Mrs. Alice "Wildie" Adams Stewart died at 9:00 a.m. on Saturday, November 15, at Wesley Memorial Hospital. There had been no surgery; she died of respiratory paralysis. The Reverend Robert Stewart was not at his wife's bedside when she succumbed to her wounds.

Alice, only 36 years old, would never see her girls grow up; she would not see Tannie or Lorene get married; she would never get to hug and kiss her grandchildren. Her life was stolen from her by moonshiners drunk on their own "shine." Her life was cut short by a sequence of events headed toward her like a run-away train. Prohibition, bootleggers, and greed took Alice's life. She was the first woman to die as a martyr after prohibition began.

After Alice passed away, Dr. Eaves called his wife, Nettie, to tell her about Alice. He asked if she knew where the pastor was. She did not. When he inquired where the daughters were, she told him that Tannie and Lorene were at the Bingham's house and that the parsonage was full of the church congregation. The parsonage had also become the headquarters of the posse.

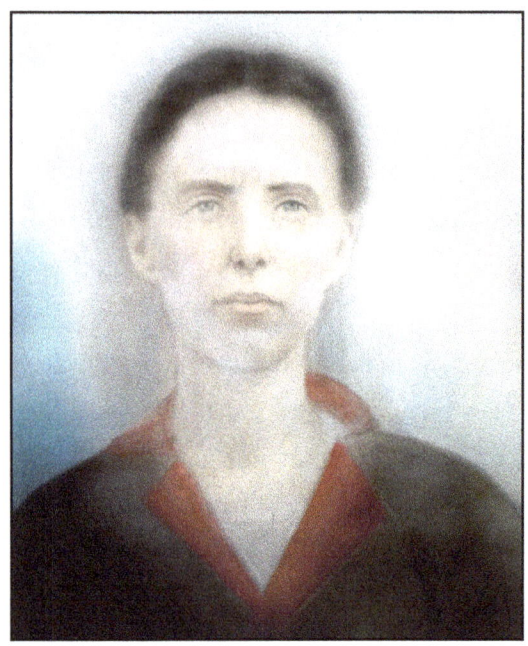

Alice "Wildie" Adams Stewart Courtesy Hazel Barnes

Eaves called the parsonage and the Sheriff's office, but was told that the sheriff and pastor were out with the posse. He left word at each place for Sheriff Richards or Reverend Stewart to call the hospital. He told no one that Alice had died. He did not want the daughters to find out from anyone except Reverend Stewart, but he realized how unrealistic this was going to be.

Eaves called his wife again. "I want you and Jesse Hogue to go to Binghams' and make sure no one comes in that house to tell them except the Reverend. Stay in their parlor and make sure no one else talks to them."

In a few hours, Reverend Stewart called the hospital and talked to Dr. Eaves and found that his wife had died. He went immediately and told his daughters.

He drove quickly to the Binghams, went bounding into the parlor, and had Melviney call up the stairway for his daughters.

When they came down the stairway, Tannie glanced at her Dad and knew. Little Lorene looked at her Dad and smiled.

"Both of you come sit by me. I've something to tell you." When they were seated on the couch beside him, he said softly, "You're mother went to live with Jesus today." Lorene put her hands over her face and began to cry, then leaned against Tannie who put her arms around her. Lorene stopped crying and looked at her dad. "That means she's not coming back?" she said struggling with the finality of death.

"Yes. Honey. She is in the arms of Jesus right now—staying with him—not coming back." He spoke these last words slowly, trailing off into realization himself.

Tannie held onto Lorene, too stricken to cry at that time. Melviney and Arreda, who stood just out of the room for them to have privacy, came in at that moment. Melviney went straight to Reverend Stewart, shaking his hand and saying, "I'm so sorry. I'm so sorry for your loss."

Arreda hugged both Lorene and then Tannie, who sat numb with shock. Since her mother was shot, she had feared her mother dying, but hoped the doctors could save her. She had looked forward to her mother coming home in a few days or a week. Now her dad told them she would never come back.

When Arreda hugged Lorene, the little girl began crying uncontrollably. Melviney took her toward the stairway to go upstairs then turned. "Pastor, I want you to stay for dinner." He nodded. The girls went upstairs, Alpha and Omega began preparing the meal, and the pastor went to the parsonage.

When the pastor went into the parsonage, he called all there to gather around and he made an announcement. "My dear wife succumbed to her wounds—shots made by these evil doers. She went to heaven this morning." The church members cried; some of the posse members left to tell others knowing efforts would be upgraded to find the culprits, and one called the sheriff's office with the news.

When Melviney was upstairs with Tannie, Lorene, and Arreda, she sat in a big chair and held Lorene. The others sat on the bed.

She told Lorene and Tannie, "You'll see your mother again. Your mother's love, laughter, and her wisdom and advice are her gifts to you. These gifts will always be with you. Being sad just means you loved her and will miss her. It's okay to be sad and cry. You'll feel better one day. Lots of people loved your mother; they will feel sad and will miss her. But we all love you and will help you through this time."

The Atlanta Constitution 11/16/1924

Stewart's two daughters stayed with the Binghams. They were in good hands. This family was a great cushion for their sorrow. The ladies of the County Line Methodist Church brought covered dishes to Melviney's kitchen, but were told that the girls were too distraught to be disturbed.

On Sunday, November 16, 1924 the front page of the Atlanta Constitution had a photograph of the Stewart family and the headlines, "2 More Arrested in Murder of Pastor's Wife." Above the featured photograph of Reverend Stewart, Lorene, and Tannie was the caption, "Family of Woman Slain by Moonshiners."

In the corner, was a picture of G. R. "Guy"

Austin who aided Reverend Stewart in his fight against moonshining. The reporters had come out to the parsonage late Saturday and made the photograph and gathered the latest information from Reverend Stewart.

Reverend Stewart resolved to push the hunt for his wife's slayers and declared that he would not give up until the last one of them had been brought to justice. Though Stewart had recognized six of the gang, he indicated close to twenty men tried to abduct him that night.

Late Sunday, when Reverend Stewart learned that John Reeves, the store owner who lived two doors down the street from the parsonage had been jailed, he called Sheriff Richards.

Over the phone, the pastor commanded, "Reeves had nothing to do with this. One of the gang stopped by the store and asked him to get me to the door, which he did. Then he went back to his store, and I came out and confronted the men in the three cars. You need to release Reeves."

With that statement, Sheriff Richards let Reeves go home to his wife and to the small community of Draketown. Richards knew that close to twenty men were in on this. He also knew that moonshine was sold right there in Draketown. He was under pressure to find those perpetrators. He needed an arrest, so he grabbed Reeves—a perfectly innocent man.

Saturday Night

Solicitor General Ed Griffith, of the Tallapoosa circuit, an active leader in the investigation of the tragedy, declared on Saturday night that he was undecided whether or not to ask the judge of the circuit to call a special term of Haralson County Court. He indicated that steps would be taken if conditions warranted it.

Tuesday, November 18th

The body of Alice "Wildie" Adams Stewart, which had been transferred on Sunday to the undertaking establishment of H. M. Patterson & Son, was then transported by Southern Railway on Tuesday to Helen Georgia, White County, for the funeral services and interment. The sorrowing husband and two daughters, Tannie and Loraine, joined the funeral party before it reached Helen. They accompanied wife and mother, Alice Adam Stewart, back to her girlhood home for the funeral service at the Chattahoochee Methodist Church Cemetery in White County near Helen.

Many members of Reverend Stewart's County Line Methodist Church congregation and some families from Draketown also took the train to attend the funeral. Members of the Bingham family—Arreda, Boots, Melviney and Jackson—rode the train, as part of the funeral group.

Chattahoochee Methodist Church, Helen, GA

A large crowd of close family members of both the Stewart family and of Alice's family, the Adams, and members from the congregation at the Chattahoochee Methodist Church attended the funeral. Arreda and her family sat in the back of the packed church.

All gathered at the graveside in reverence and support of Alice Stewart and her family. Arreda stood where she could see Lorene and only once did Lorene look toward her to know she was there. Arreda raised her hand and gave a slight wave to the sorrow-struck six-year-old. Lorene smiled at her between her tears.

Attending the graveside were a large number of Ku Klux Klan members. These Klan members were devoted to justice and to support Reverend Robert Stewart's movement against the making, distributing, and drinking of alcoholic beverages. The Klan, in their white robes, stood in reverence on the mountainous hillside among the towering oak trees beside the picturesque old church as a show of their loyalty to the Stewart family.

Cemetery on hillside, Courtesy Harold McCay

After the burial, Stewart left the grave of his wife and returned to Haralson

County to join in the hunt for the alleged members of the gang.

Stewart's daughters returned to Haralson County. Even though they still lived in the parsonage, they stayed with the Binghams and only went home to get clothes. The members of the congregation came by the Bingham's occasionally to bring food and to encourage the daughters.

Sheriff Richards and his deputies continued to scour the mountainous sections of Haralson County for the four men who were named in warrants as having been the moonshiners who had planned to abduct and pistol-whip the pastor.

Wednesday, November 19th

Six days after Alice Stewart had been shot, ten men had been arrested and were in jail at Buchanan: Joe Cash, and Tom Gather were the first arrested; then, Tom Barber, about sixteen, of Draketown; Pete Barber of Draketown was next; then, warrants were sworn out by Reverend Stewart and his daughters for James Hendrix, about fifty, and his two sons, Hurbert and Owen, both under twenty; Stan Hester about sixteen who lived in Paulding County; and Everett Holder of Paulding County; plus George Hudson, age fifty, who had recently moved to Rockmart. In a few days, the last of these men were arrested and taken to the Buchanan jail.

Buchanan was crowded with visitors, many who were related to the accused men.

All these men declared innocence and declared they could establish alibis. These would-be assailants were guarded with strictest secrecy.

A preliminary hearing was set for the next day—Thursday, November 20th. These ten men would appear before a judge to find if there was enough evidence for a trial. The Solicitor General, Edward Griffith, planned a special term of court starting in January 1925, to try the prisoners in the event that charges were preferred against them.

Most of the shadows of this life are caused
by our standing in our own sunshine.
                    Ralph Waldo Emerson.

Chapter 8
The Community and State Reacts

January 1989

At the beauty shop in Villa Rica, while Arreda got a perm, she told Trisha and those other patrons listening about the reaction of the neighbors after Alice's death.

"Jesse Hogue, who lived across the street, saw it all happen. She was Alice's best friend. They worked together almost daily to help the people in the community someway. They went to visit the sick; have prayer, and carry food they had prepared."

"When old man Lambert's porch fell in and he couldn't get in the door or out the door, they found someone in Draketown to go rebuild it for him. Alice asked the lumber mill in Cedartown to donate the boards and a hardware store in Draketown to donate the nails. Of course they donated these things because it was Alice Stewart asking. Everyone loved and admired her. Everyday the two of them were out doing good somewhere to help somebody."

"After Jesse saw Alice shot that night, she was in a state—she just walked from window to window looking out and singing hymns softly. I guess that's how she dealt with the pain she felt inside."

"For weeks after Alice died, people came by the parsonage to stand outside and share stories of how she helped them or their neighbor or relative.

Alice Stewart's death and the circumstances surrounding her murder outraged the people in Draketown, the people across the county, and the people across the state. National newspaper coverage, especially in the South, drew attention to the case. Newspapers around the country carried the news of a pastor's wife being assassinated and presented details of Stewart's warfare on alcohol:

"Stewart had waged unceasing warfare on the liquor-runners and rum-makers of Haralson County. As a result, he had incurred bitter enemies among them and had been repeatedly warned to cease his activities. On Sunday, he administered the Gospel to his flock, but on the other six days of the week he spent much time scouring the county for stills and liquor-runners, with a big revolver hanging from a cartridge-filled belt around his waist. He had been responsible for the breaking up of countless stills and seizure of a large quantity of liquor."

The Ku Klux Klan Sponsors a Parade

As the death of Alice Stewart became publicized locally and even nationally, support also came from a rather unlikely source—the Ku Klux Klan. The Klan put out the word, all over, "We had nothing to do with the attempted abduction of Reverend Stewart and we had nothing to do with the shooting of his wife, Alice Stewart."

The Tallapoosa Ku Klux Klan passed strong resolutions condemning the perpetrators of the crime which had so stirred the South, pledging its support to the officers in the upholding of the law.

The Tallapoosa Klan passed the following resolution, adopted by John B. Gordon, Klan, Number Two, Realm of Georgia.

"Whereas a most brutal murder has been committed in our county by cowardly weaklings and treacherous scalawags, moonshiners and bootleggers in open defiance of the constitution and laws of our government both federal and state who deceitfully decoyed the Reverend Robert Stewart from his home and attempted to carry him away in automobiles. When his wife came to his rescue she was shot down practically in the door of her home by this brutal mob.

"Secondly, to the Reverend Robert Stewart and family, we extend our sympathy. To the Sheriff and legally constituted officers, we pledge our aid and support in running down the perpetrators of this dastardly deed and putting them in the custody of the law where just punishment shall be meted out to each of them.

"Third, believing the Reverend Robert Stewart a man actuated by manly motives and personally aspiring to all things noble for himself and humanity, as proven by the active patriotic duties he has so well exemplified in the past, we as Klansmen assembled, commend and appreciate the active patriotic services and (illegible) example of good that he has preached from his pulpit and practiced among his fellows in his daily walk of life."

On November 23, 1924, the Sunday following Alice Stewart's funeral, the

Tallapoosa Ku Klux Klan sponsored a twenty-one car caravan carrying loads of Klansmen, in full regalia, to visit the little Methodist parsonage at Draketown. The Klansmen from Bremen, Tallapoosa, and Waco presented Robert Stewart with $50 and a commitment to support the lawmen's efforts in finding the killer or killers. They extended to the bereaved pastor the profound sympathy of the Klan in his bereavement.

The procession began at Tallapoosa, passed through Waco and Bremen, and on to Draketown. The return trip was made through Buchanan. The leading car carried a big American flag.

On Sunday afternoon, when the parade came down the one street in Draketown, Main Street, it created a spectacle. Everyone came out to observe and stand along side the road. The flags waved in the cool November air. Family members rode in the cars.

Boots Bingham, who was on the front porch at the Bingham house, ran in and called to everyone, "Come quick. There's a parade of the Klan coming through Draketown!"

When the twenty-one cars came slowly up Temple Road from the south and turned onto the main road through town. The lead car continued to the west end of town. The other cars came in behind, clogging the Main Road past the curve of the town on the east. Everyone looked to see the leaders who carried the flag; they were walking back to the parsonage.

By this time, Boots had gone over to the parsonage to alert the pastor who had just come from church with his daughters. He knocked on the door; the three of them grabbed their coats and were on the porch by the time the Klan leaders made their way to Reverend Stewart's home.

"Pastor," one called out. "We have brought you a gift."

For whatever Reverend Stewart had thought, he looked visibly relieved. Tannie was terrified and stepped back into the front room. Boots looked surprised that she had gone back inside and went with her to watch from the window as she sat huddled in the corner of the sofa.

Lorene stood fast with her father, taking it all in.

"We have $50 to give you and your family as condolences for the tragic death of your wife."

Three tall Klansmen in their full regalia stood on the porch towering over

Reverend Stewart and little Lorene. They each shook his hand; one patted Lorene on the head. They handed Reverend Stewart an envelope containing $50 cash.

Reverend Robert Stewart Courtesy Hazel Barnes

"This is from our members to let you know we grieve for your loss."

Arreda had come up on the porch to stand beside Lorene and watch the tall white-robed men with the tall white hoods shake hands with Reverend Stewart, give him the envelope, then leave.

The two young girls ran inside and upstairs to Lorene's room. They went immediately to the bedroom window to watch the line of cars drive away. Arreda asked, "You weren't afraid of the Klan in their robes?"

"Nah. I know some of them. They come to the parsonage to see Daddy all the time. I recognized Mr. Smith's voice—it's real deep. Mr. Eddy's voice is high and kinda squeaky like this—*HELLO LITTLE GIRL, HOW ARE YOU?*" They both giggled.

"Mr. Hooper wears those same brown shoes with the tassels. He's the one who gave Daddy the money just now. When he's here, they talk about how the Klan helps to enforce the law."

Lorene continued, "I'm not afraid of the Klan members. The parade was kinda nice. Even though they looked kinda scary in their long white robes and pointed hats when they walked down the line of cars to our house. I saw in each car their wife and kids were with them. I go to school with a few of those kids."

Lorene and Arreda talked as they stood in her window, looking down at the cars with the robed members of the Klan and their families leaving Draketown.

Suddenly Lorene lowered her voice to nearly a whisper and said, "I never told anyone this before." Arreda looked at here inquisitively.

"One day I looked under the bed in Mother and Daddy's room. I was looking for my ball. I saw a box under there. I got the box from under the bed and opened it. It had a white Klan robe in it. I quickly put the lid back on and put it back under the bed. I never told Daddy I found it. I figured it was a secret. I never told anyone, until now, not even Mother or Tannie." She sighed.

The young girls watched the cars leave town until the last car passed. The street was clear now, all the way down to the big curve; they would never forget what they saw.

Tannie sat on the sofa, shaking. Boots had come back inside also, but now he stood at the window and watched them leave.

As Pastor Stewart came in, Boots asked, "Can Tannie come have dessert with us—we're having rice puddin'?"

The Reverend looked up as though he had been unaware of the two of them and nodded. He seemed deep in thought.

Boots and Tannie were out the front door, down the street, and to the Bingham's front porch in no time.

Tannie & Lorene, Courtesy Hazel Barnes

"Tannie, why were you so scared of the Klan? They were only here to show support and give your Dad the money."

Tannie took a seat in the rocking chair which sat in the warm sunlight. "I saw what happened to my mother," she replied. "When I heard the first shots, I ran to the window—my bedroom is the one on the left, upstairs. I was right over them, in line with the last two cars. I saw a guy get out of the car. He wore a hood, not the full robe, just the hood. He shot at my mother after she had shot twice toward them. When the shots were fired, for a split second, I could see the surroundings. Mama was hit and fell on the ground and he shot her again. When he did, he took off his hood and turned toward the car behind him to get in and leave."

"As he turned, I could tell it was Stan Hester. The light from the lamp in the window downstairs cast just enough light that I could tell who he was. I went to school with Stan. I know that was Stan. But when I try to tell Daddy that some of the men in the third car wore hoods, he told me to forget what I saw. He told me that he was in charge of the situation and knows what to do for the good of everyone. I am so confused."

Boots, who had propped up against the porch post beside the rocker where

Tannie had told her story, replied, "I don't understand why some moonshiners wore Klan hoods. I thought a moonshiner gang came after your daddy because he had torn down their stills. I also thought the Klan supported prohibition. That's what my daddy said."

"Exactly," replied Tannie. "I'm so confused. Then why did all these Klan members bring us money today and act so sorry as they shook hands with my daddy?"

"What I can't understand," Boots said rubbing his neck and looking perplexed, "is why Stan Hester had a Klan hood. He's only 16. He's my age. What is he doing with a Klan Hood? Where did he get it? He's *not* in the Klan. And what about the others you saw in the third car? I wonder if they really represented the Klan or were they just borrowing the hoods so they would not be recognized?"

"Could be." Tannie had a far-away look. "Or maybe some of these so-called righteous Klan members might be moonshiners also."

Boots was thoughtful. "Daddy said now that there are prohibition laws, more people drink more liquor and whisky than they ever did, just on the sly. I'm sure some of the Klan members take a drink of illegal whisky, without being moonshiners belonging to a gang."

At that moment, Melviney called them from the doorway, "Y'all better come in and have some rice puddin'."

Reward of $200 Offered by the Governor of Georgia

The Governor of Georgia, Clifford Walker, who was in attendance at a conference of governors held in Jacksonville, Florida, wired authorization for a reward of $200 to be offered to any person with information that would lead to the arrest and conviction of each of the unknown parties who had been part in the gang who shot and killed Mrs. Alice Stewart of Draketown.

Two-hundred dollars was more money than some farmers made in a year in 1924.

The Secretary of State Made it Formal

"I, S. G. McLendon, Secretary of State, do hereby issue this my Proclamation offering a reward of Two Hundred Dollars for the apprehension and delivery of Unknown Parties, official information having been received that on November 13. 1924, Mrs. Robert Stewart, residing in Draketown, Haralson County, was brutally shot down by Unknown Parties who have escaped and are now fugitives from justice, with evidence sufficient to convict, to the Sheriff of Haralson County State of Georgia. And I do, moreover, charge and require all officers in this state, Civil and Military, to be vigilant endeavoring to apprehend the said Unknown Parties in order that he may be brought to trial for the offense with which he stands charged. Given under my hand and seal of office, this the 20th day of November 1924. S. G. McLendon Secretary of State."

The Haralson County Solicitor General, Edward S. Griffith of the Tallapoosa Circuit, requested the posting of the rewards and declared that he would do everything possible to find and convict the slayers.

The Georgia Baptist Convention

The Georgia Baptist Convention, in final session on November 20th, one week after the attack at the parsonage in Draketown, adopted a resolution deploring the attempt at moonshiners and bootleggers to kidnap Reverend Robert Stewart, a Methodist pastor, and 'the cruel murder' of his dauntless wife. The resolution called the incident only a climax of crime caused by lax enforcement of law, by convert and sometimes expressed sympathies for violators of prohibition and other laws by some city, county and state officials and leading citizens.

Small fines instead of prison sentences were condemned in the resolution as being 'a travesty on law and an encouragement to crime as heard by grand juries and law associations.' These small fines instead of prison sentences are most often given by certain judicial officers to those who are convicted or who plead guilty, now a common custom as the easiest way out, such judicial leniency being a travesty on law and an encouragement to crime as asserted by grand juries and law associations. It was asserted in the Baptists' resolution that many prominent citizens, including church members 'scout the law, patronize moonshiners, and boast of their bootleggers.'

The resolutions urged that all citizens obey the law and "that our newspapers, magazines and moving pictures commend and not condemn the law." It further urged sheriffs, policemen, and others "to enforce the laws without fear or favor and all our pastors to preach often on the necessity of law enforcement by all officers and law observance by all citizens. We respectfully suggest that our churches observe by special programs the Sabbath preceding January 16, 1925, the fifth anniversary of the 18th amendment."

North Georgia Methodist Conference

In a sermon at Druid Hills Methodist church Sunday morning, Dr. Elam F. Dempsey, secretary of education for the North Georgia Methodist Conference, denounced "the lawlessness, liquor manufacturing and liquor-drinking that is responsible for the crime."

Speaking of Alice Stewart, Dr. Dempsey said: "She was such a wife as that the heart of her husband safely trusted in her, and she was such a mother, too, as that her children could not but rise up and call her blessed. Robert Stewart, man of God, my fellow minister in the Methodist itinerancy, and a fearless citizen of my state, was my neighbor in a former charge. At this hour, as I speak of him, knowing him as warmhearted and as tender as he is brave, I feel that if I would fittingly speak of him, it would be in words of flame hissing through a bath of tears—flame of holy hate—tears of sacred sorrow, and divine compassions."

"One such man and one such woman are more to be deserved than all the bootleggers, rum-runners and whisky-smugglers that ever were spawned or ever will be spawned in the hell of greed, debauchery and lawlessness."

"Not once, but twice in our Georgia history have such heroines illustrated our annals with wifely loyalty and motherly bravery. Mrs. Stewart's name deserves to be written alongside that of Grace Darling and all such heroines. While there are such women left among us, from whom American youths may be born, and at whose breasts they may be nourished, we need not marvel at the heroism of Belleau Wood and Chateau Thierty, which makes America illustrious for bravery, for she is the bravest of the brave."

"Coming of a race who wrought out the law of habeas corpus, securing the sacredness of the person, and who had taught all men to know that every home, whether palace, lowly cottage or humble Methodist parsonage—is every man's castle, her gallant rush to her husband's relief, when assaulted by hoodlums, was as natural as it was for her to breathe. Glorious, brave mother, dauntless mate and wife—we have no material fit for your monument and no words adequate in memorialize your greatness!

Dr. Dempsey announced Friday night that memorial services would be held throughout Georgia the next Sunday morning.

Bronze Memorial Marker

The Atlanta Constitution, November 24, 1924: *A special collection will be taken to place a bronze tablet in Wesley Memorial Hospital and to provide funds to aid wives of Methodist Ministers who become patients at the hospital. The memorial committee, headed by Mrs. A. F. Nunn, wife of the Methodist pastor at Temple, is asking all churches in the conference to pay tribute to the "woman who gave her life for the enforcement of laws of the nation." Other members of the committee are Mrs. W. T. Irvine, of Rome, and Mrs. Warren A. Candler, of Atlanta. The proposition to honor Mrs. Stewart was presented at the annual conference of the North Georgia Methodist conference. U. V. W. Darlington, presiding and other leaders gave their hearty support.*

More than 500 letters have been sent to women in the conference by the committee asking cooperation in making the memorial a "spiritual as well as a financial success."

Mrs. Robert Stewart Memorial

Martyr blood should not be shed in vain.

Mrs. Robert Stewart, brave martyr to love and law enforcement, is too lofty a spirit to be memorialized by any material monument. Service alone is a fit memorial to such a soul.

Mrs. A. F. Nunn, wife of a neighboring itinerate Methodist preacher, has suggested that a bronze tablet with suitable inscription be placed in the main hall of Wesley Memorial Hospital and that a fund be raised by free-will offerings of women, income from which shall be used to furnish comforts, special services, et., to all wives of itinerates who may hereafter become patients in Wesley Memorial hospital. Mail gifts or subscriptions to Mrs. A. F. Nunn, Temple, Ga.

PLEDGE OR CASH OFFERING

I hearby (enclose $_____) (subscribe $_____) as my gift to the "Mrs. Robert Stewart Memorial Fund."

Name_____Street_____

City_____State_____

Make checks payable to Mrs. A. F. Nunn, Temple, Ga.

Memorial Service

The Atlanta Constitution, November 29, 1924, stated: All the Methodist Episcopal churches of north Georgia will observe this Sunday as "Mrs. Robert Stewart Memorial Day." Offerings will be taken during the service for Mrs. Stewart's memorial which it is proposed to establish at Wesley Memorial hospital. The campaign is being directed by Dr. E. F. Dempsey of Atlanta. Checks for the memorial fund should be payable to Mrs. A. F. Nunn of Temple who conceived the idea of the memorial.

The Memorial Service was held on a December Sunday night at Wesley Memorial Church with special music and a special program. Among the speakers were representatives of Woman's Christian Temperance Union of Georgia and Dr. C. O. Jones, Superintendent of the Georgia Department of the Anti-Saloon League.

In a December 1, 1924 letter to Robert Stewart, Marvin Williams, Pastor of Wesley Memorial Methodist Church stated:

Dear Brother Stewart:

As you may have heard it announced at Conference we are to have a Memorial Service next Sunday night. We are hoping to make this a great occasion and to glorify the brave death of your wife as a deed in the great cause. If you can give us the main facts about her, her maiden name, where you all were married and how long she has been a Preacher's wife. Give any facts about her that you think would be of interest. If you can do this I will appreciate it.

Also tell me anything you can about your efforts to down bootlegging which led to this tragedy.

I am praying and believing that your brave wife will accomplish more by her death than most women do by their entire lives. It is surprising and gratifying how they are taking hold of this movement in various forms all over the state.

Kindly let me hear from you at your earliest convenience and if you come to Atlanta come by to see me.

Sincerely, Marvin Williams

Tallapoosa Woman's Christian Temperance Union Makes a Strong Stand For Law Enforcement

December 11, 1924: The Haralson Times announced: *At a recent meeting of the Tallapoosa W. C. T. U., the following strong resolutions were unanimously adopted:*

First: That the representing American womanhood deplore the conditions that necessitate the sacrifice of a woman's life in defense of her husband and home.

Second: That as an organization we stand for the observance and enforcement of law, especially the Eighteenth Amendment.

Third: That we stand by our courts and our officers in their efforts to enforce law, and in using our rights of franchise will do all in our power to put in office such men as will do this.

Fourth: That copies of this resolution be furnished our county papers and a copy sent to Solicitor E. S. Griffith.

Georgia Woman's Christian Temperance Union. January 1, 1925

Alice Stewart, the first woman martyr to the cause of prohibition, was honored in state-wide memorial services held by Law Enforcement on January 1, 1925, on New Year's night. Each of these memorial services were sponsored by the local W. C. T. U. in all sections of the state.

> *"The world cries loud for blood.*
> *There never grew one saving*
> *Truth that blossomed, man to bless.*
> *That withered not in barren loneliness*
> *'Til watered by the sacrificial dew."*

The program on New Year's night 1925 included patriotic songs, scripture readings and brief talks on "The First Woman Martyr," "The Menace of Lawlessness," and The Stewart Living Memorial," and a reading, "Killing the Dragon." These meetings had been preceded by a day of prayer and fasting by W. C. T. U. members.

Resolutions for adoption at these law enforcement meetings ends with: "We urge all citizens to obey the law; our newspapers and magazines and moving pictures to commend and not condemn the law; our judges to discourage liquor violations by placing sentences to the full extent of the law, viz: prison sentences after the second offense instead of any fines; our sheriffs policemen and others to enforce the law fearlessly; and all pastors to preach often on the necessity of law enforcement by all officers and law observance by all citizens; that communities see to it that all members of juries are clean, upright, law-abiding citizens and in no way in sympathy with the liquor traffic by reason of business or social affiliation with these enemies to all righteous laws."

The Stewart Living Memorial

Mary Harris Armour in the Georgia Woman's Christian Temperance Union, President's Newsletter for the new year of 1925, called for the Stewart Living Memorial be set up: "Be thou faithful unto death and I will give thee a crown of life," is the promise, and as year after year on the 13th of November (the anniversary of Alice Stewart's tragic attack), we shall gather in every city and town in this state to hold memorial law enforcement or law observance meetings; we will take an offering at each of these meetings to be used by the Georgia W. C. T. U. for organization work. Suggestive programs have been sent to every local president for this 'memorial law enforcement meeting.'"

". . . your brave wife will accomplish more by her death than most women do by their entire lives. It is surprising and gratifying how they are taking hold of this movement in various forms all over the state."
Dr. Elam F. Dempsey

Chapter 9
Lies and Alibis

Preliminary Trial at the Haralson County Courthouse

Thursday, November 20, 1924, one week after Alice Stewart was shot, a preliminary hearing was held at the Haralson County Courthouse in Buchanan, the County Seat of Haralson County. Ten men were brought before Judge F. A. Irwin of the Tallapoosa Circuit.

Farmers and residents from all parts of Haralson County dropped their work and began pouring into Buchanan. By the hour the hearing was scheduled to begin, the greatest crowd ever gathered within the limits of the small town of Buchanan was waiting in or near the courthouse.

Reverend Robert Stewart and his two daughters, Tannie and Loraine, would appear as principal witnesses.

During this hearing, Reverend Robert Stewart, Methodist preacher and liquor raider, in whose defense Mrs. Stewart died, mounted the witness stand and described in graphic detail the events leading up to the tragic death of his wife.

When Reverend Robert Stewart testified, he told in detail the events that took place on the night his wife was shot. Upon direct examination by Solicitor Griffith, Stewart said he recognized James Hendrix and his two sons, Hurbert and Owen, as well as Tate Gather and Pete Barber. He also declared that Stan Hester—the first man he saw of the gang—was the man who fired one of the shots that took his wife's life. On cross-examination his story remained unshaken.

Mrs. Jesse Hogue Testifies

Mrs. Jesse Hogue, wife of the physician who was one of the first to reach Mrs. Stewart's side on the night of the shooting, insisted on reading passages of Scripture and praying before testifying.

Old Buchanan Courthouse, built 1891

She first asked permission to "make a little statement." The solicitor told her to take the stand and proceed.

"I have never been in court before," Mrs. Hogue began, "but I never undertake anything without first invoking the blessing of Almighty God." Mrs. Hogue read several passages of Scripture and in the course of her fervent prayer, she said:

"May the blood of all officers in the state boil until they wipe out this whisky evil, so defenseless women may not be called out in the dead of the night and be killed in cold blood."

Judge Irwin made no effort to interrupt Mrs. Hogue. The courtroom echoed a nervous shuffling of feet by the spectators as the little woman began her prayer. When she finished, she announced her readiness for the questioning process. Mrs. Hogue's testimony corroborated that of the preacher. Her husband was called to the stand shortly afterward, telling substantially the same story.

Dr. Eaves Testifies

Dr. B. F. Eaves, the next witness called by the state, told how he rushed to Mrs. Stewart's side soon after she was wounded and of the hurried trip in his automobile to an Atlanta hospital where she died two days later.

"When I last saw Mrs. Stewart alive," the physician said, "she told me she had something of importance to say. She drew my head down and in a weak whisper said: 'Pete Barber was one of the men I saw in the automobile before I was shot.'

He testified also that both shots which struck Mrs. Stewart's elbow and spinal column were fired from the rear of the line of three automobiles.

Sheriff George B. Richards

Sheriff George B. Richards, a man of few words who was plain spoken and quietly intelligent, was called to the stand where he testified of his visit to the Atlanta Hospital to hear Alice Stewart's death bed testimony that she recognized Pete Barber as one of the men in the gang that night.

He presented her version of what happened to the court: "Alice Stewart was gravely ill and very weak, but she was in her right mind when she told me what happened; I can quote because I wrote down everything she told me word for word."

"Alice had whispered to me, 'After we retired on Thursday night, three cars loaded with men drove up to our home and called for my husband. He immediately left the house and started toward the cars, but as he neared them he apparently recognized some of the men, for he hesitated. Then they seized him and attempted to push him into a car. Seeing the apparent danger he was in, I grabbed his gun and rushed out. The men had pushed him into a car, gagged him and was in the process of binding his wrists and ankles. I called out for them to release him. I pleaded, Please let him go. Then I fired aiming low trying to hit their knees. After I fired, someone shot me. I don't remember anything after that until I woke up here in the hospital.'"

Sheriff Richards repeated what the doctors had told him. "Mrs. Stewart had been shot twice, one bullet entered her right elbow; a second bullet was fired striking her in the back at the spinal column and ranging upward puncturing several vertebrae."

John R. Reeves' Testimony

John R. Reeves, Draketown merchant, testified, "the automobiles stopped in front of the Methodist parsonage at about 8:00 oclock Thursday night. I operate a general store next door to the parsonage. A tall man in a dark hat came into my store. I was surprised. It was late. I was about to lock up. He asked me to call Reverend Stewart out. I did. Then I went back into my store and my wife and I watched. The minister, who had retired, dressed and approached the middle automobile which contained six men."

"When the minister hesitated, he was grabbed by some of the men and upon his outcry his wife appeared on the scene, rushing from the house in her nightgown, pistol in hand."

"This plucky little woman fired two shots into the crowd of night riders before a shot from the automobile knocked her to the ground. Then one of the cowards rushed up to her and fired another shot into her body as she lay upon the ground."

Reeves continued, "In the confusion occasioned by Mrs. Stewart's appearance upon the scene, the minister was liberated and the cars beat a hasty retreat."

Solicitor Griffith

Solicitor Griffith began, " The rumor is current that some of the party was struck by the bullets fired by Mrs. Stewart, but thus far there has been no developments to substantiate this claim."

Two of the Men are Freed

Two men were given their freedom—Joe Cash of Polk County, and George Hudson of Rockmart were released because of lack of evidence.

Eight of the ten men arrested were called to come before the grand jury on charges of murder in connection with the slaying of Mrs. Robert Stewart at Draketown. They were James Hendrix and his sons, Owen and Hurbert Hendrix, Stan Hester, and Everett Holder of Paulding County, Tom Barber of Draketown; Pete Barber of Draketown, and Tate Gather of Draketown.

Two More Men and Stan Hester are Freed

The Atlanta Constitution: *Stan Hester—the man who was declared by Mr. Stewart to have fired one of the fatal shots, has been released from the Haralson County jail. Tom Barber and Everette Holder were given their freedom at the same time.*

Stan Hester's release by the authorities created a sensation since Reverend Stewart testified that he positively recognized Stan Hester as one of the men who shot Mrs. Stewart. Ed Griffith, solicitor general of the Tallapoosa court, explained that the three men had put up irrefutable alibis and on that account had been released. He states, however, that their release did not exempt them from indictment by the grand jury or from further arrest.

Tom Barber

When Tom and Pete were arrested in the barn, Tom had been released immediately. He showed the sheriff the injury on his neck and told how he had been plowing a field for next spring—getting the ground ready.

"I had put the straps around my neck while I unhitched the mule. That ole' jackass took a step forward and nearly broke my neck. There was no way in the world I was in that gang. I was home with Mama who rubbed liniment on my neck for days. There was several days I could not even move my neck from side to side."

Tom leaned his head forward and pulled the neck of his shirt back to reveal a large, red raw-looking area on the back of his neck. Tom straightened up and adjusted his shirt.

The sheriff regarded Tom for several minutes. "How old are you, Tom?"

"Sir, I'm only sixteen. But I'm big for my age and I can do as much work as any man, any day of the week."

"Well son, if you ever put the straps around your neck again, you might not live to be a man. I hope you have learned a lesson."

"Oh yes Sir, I have." Tom rubbed his neck and walked quickly away. Tom talked his way out of this situation. The injury on his neck was because the third car he was driving had been shot and the glass had cut through his shirt.

November 27, The Haralson County Tribune, Grand Jury Likely to be Called in Session

A special session of the grand jury will be called, beginning in January 1925, to investigate the charges against five men held in the county jail in connection with the fatal shooting of Mrs. Robert Stewart which occurred at Draketown on November 13th.

The Haralson County Tribune, December 1924, Sheriff and Posse Destroy Nine Giant Stills Saturday; 4 Men are Captured in Raid

Sheriff G. B. Richards, together with Deputy Swint and Constable Raymer Mize and J. W. Williams of this county, and Deputy Sheriff Owens, of Cleburne County, Ala., made a rich haul Saturday when they captured and destroyed nine giant illicit distilleries, all of which were located just over the line in Alabama.

Five of these stills were of 600 gallon capacity each, while the remaining four were estimated as having a capacity of from two to four hundred gallons. Four men were captured in the raid, two by the name of Hicksley and two men named Cash. 25 gallons of booze were also captured and destroyed.

These distilleries had apparently been operating for some time and must have turned out thousands of gallons of whisky before being destroyed. They were all with-

in one-half to a mile of the state line, but everyone of them was in Alabama. Alabama officials had been prevented from patrolling that section for some time past owing to the bad condition of the roads.

The moonshining business in Haralson County has been pretty well cleared up, most illicit whisky consumed in this county coming from across the line in Alabama and Haralson officials will watch the state line operations, who send their vile stuff to this county.

The Atlanta Constitution, January 21, 1925, Grand Jury Considers Stewart Case Wednesday Indictments Are Sought

Buchanan, Ga. The grand jury is expected to consider Wednesday the cases of the five men held in connection with the death of Mrs. Robert Stewart, who was shot down at Draketown . . .

Superior Court opened here Monday, with Judge Frank A. Irvin, presiding and Ed Griffith representing the state, as solicitor general. Reverend Stewart has since been transferred to a charge at Greensboro, (Green County) Ga.

The Atlanta Constitution January 30, 1925: Stewart Case Set For Next Monday

On account of bad weather and roads preventing the appearing of witnesses, the Stewart case was today postponed 'til next Monday, February 2. . . . Robert Stewart is here to assist in avenging the death of his wife. More that 200 witnesses, it is said, have been summoned.

The Atlanta Constitution February 1, 1925, Trial at Buchanan of Stewart Case

. . . The five men who go on trial were held at a preliminary trial following the death of Mrs. Stewart and were indicted last week by the grand jury. . . .

Grand Jury Trial: January Term, 1925
The State of Georgia, Haralson County: True Bill #64

The Grand Jurors, selected, chosen, and sworn for the County of Haralson to wit: J. L. Bailey, M. T. Baskin, W. P. Baxter, H. P. Blackman, R. A. Chandler, S. L. Gable, J. V. Hart, A. A. Hurst, E. Jaillet, L. J. Jeffers, W. L. Long, J. A. Newman, R. F. Otwell, David Peyton, J. H. Price, E. A. Pope, William A. Sayer, T. J. Tillman, H. T. Tuck, M. W. Weatherby, John S. Westbrooks, and J. W. Williams, .

Draketown Tragedy

In the name and behalf of the citizens of Georgia, charge and accuse: the The Grand Juror: State vs. James Hendrix, Hurbert Hendrix, Owen Hendrix, Charles "Pete" Barber and Tate Gather of the County and State aforesaid, with the offense of murder. For that the said James Hendrix, Hurbert Hendrix, Owen Hendrix, Charles "Pete" Barber and Tate Gather on the 13th day of November, in the year of our Lord 1924, in the county aforesaid did then and there unlawfully, and with forethought and arms, make and assault in and upon one, **Mrs. Robert Stewart**, in the peace of God and said State then and there being then and there unlawfully feloniously, wilfully and of this malice aforethought, **did kill and murder by shooting the said Mrs. Robert Stewart** with a certain pistol another firearm to Grand Jurors unknown a further description of said weapon to Grand jurors unknown which the said James Hendrix, Hurbert Hendrix, Owen Hendrix, Pete Barber, and Tate Gather then and there held, and giving to, the said Mrs. Robert Stewart, then and there a mortal wound, of which mortal wound the said Mrs. Robert Stewart died, and so the jurors aforesaid upon their oath aforesaid, so say that the said O. J. Hendrix, Hurbert Hendrix, Owen Hendrix, Pete Barber, and Tate Gather the said Mrs. Robert Stewart in manner and form aforesaid unlawfully feloniously wilfully and of their malice aforethought, did kill and murder, contrary to the laws of said state, the good order, peace and dignity thereof.

Prosecutor: Robert Stewart

Sol. Gen. E. S. Griffith

Witnesses: Robert Stewart, G. B. Richards, W. H. Swint, J. W. Wyatt, Foster Meeks, Floyd McClendon, Dr. B. F. Eaves, Dr. W. L. Hogue, Owen Tyson, Munral Swafford, Glenn Cole, Glynn Cook, Gladys Cole, Gail Cook, Mrs. W. L. Hogue, J. M. Goldin, Jim Taylor, Loyd Bagget, J. R. Reeves.

Foreman: J. W. Williams

Special presentment

Prosecutor E. S. Griffith, assistant in prosecution: Will Trawick of Cedartown

Clerk: J. R. Brown

Attorneys for the defense: J. R. Hutcheson of Douglasville, Walter Matthews, Buchanan, and R. S. McGarity of Dallas Ga.

The Atlanta Constitution, February 3, 1925: Four More Arrested as Seven More are Sought

As the first day of trial began, it was announced that four more men had been arrested in December and a search was underway for seven others. Because of the tireless search for evidence on the part of Sheriff G. B. Richardson, Deputy Sheriff Henry Swint, Special Deputy Ben Smith of Tallapoosa, and others, four more men were now in the clutches of the law. These alleged members of the mob who had been arrested late in December of 1924 are: Ben Cash, Jim Cash, Harry Hicksley, and Emmett Hicksley. All four of these men lived near the scene of the killing. These four were arrested just over the Haralson County line and were taken to the Tallapoosa jail. It was hoped that one of the men would give a confession of the attempted kidnapping of Reverend Stewart and of the shooting of Mrs. Stewart.

The Atlanta Constitution, February 3, 1925: Men Identified in Stewart Case

Every available officer and volunteer willing to bring justice to the state of Georgia has been dispatched on a rapid search for seven other men alleged to have been members of the mob who visited the home of the pastor. The arrest of these four men is said to have come as a result of a full statement by a Paulding County man who counts himself familiar with the whole circumstances.

Coming in the midst of the trial of the five men, who were arrested immediately after the murder and who have been in the Buchanan jail since, the arrest of four and the search for seven has brought a renewed interest to the sensational trial underway at the Buchanan Courthouse. Hundreds of people have been assembled since Monday morning to witness the proceedings and to hear the evidence.

Trial of James Hendrix, Tuesday, February 3, 1925

The trial was held at the Old Buchanan Courthouse. This second floor courtroom was a large room with a raised judge's stand in the front center of the room and an elevated jury platform with twelve captain-style, swivel chairs for each of the jury members. There were long benches on each side of a center aisle and side aisles which led to the door at the back and split stairways on each side of a landing that led down to the first floor.

Some of the Bingham family attended the trial. On the morning of the trial Arreda, who took off school that day, sat with her parents, Jackson and Melviney. It was decided between the Reverend Stewart and the Binghams, that it would be better for Lorene to stay with Alpha and Omega who did not attend the trial. Both Jackson and Bud attended to hear the proceedings as there was no work at the grist mill in the winter.

Tannie, who rode into Buchanan that morning with the Binghams, approached her father before court began. She told her father once again that she saw Stan Hester shoot her mother. She told him that Stan Hester wore a white-pointed hood like a Klan hood. After he shot her mother, he took the hood off as he turned to enter the third car which then sped away. She told him she stood in the window on the second floor which put her several feet above and a short distance away from the cars and the men. She said she counted the men and that some had on the pointed white hoods of the Klan.

As Reverend Stewart listened to his daughter describe what she remembered, his eyes glared almost hatred and his face turned crimson when he said, in a controlled anger so that the veins of his neck popped out, "Young Lady, don't you ever say anything like that again. If you think you saw the Klan, you are mistaken. Some of them probably wore pillow-slips over their heads, so as not to be recognized. I know what I'm doing. This is not to be repeated, ever."

When Tannie spoke to Sheriff Richards without her father knowing, he looked very thoughtful and was quiet for a few moments, before he spoke.

"Tannie, you've been through a shock. No one should ever have to see what you did. I think you are still in a state of shock. I have to believe Reverend Stewart, that he knows what is the best to be told. He has to think of what's best for the most people. What he said is the truth, backed up by Mr. and Mrs. Reeves. They were there. They saw what happened. They did not mention anyone wearing a hood of any kind."

Tannie returned, "John and Pearl were in the doorway of the store. They were too far away to see that several members of the Klan were in the third car and too far away to know that one of the men got out and shot my mother, took the hood off and got back into the car. I was just several feet above him. It was Stan Hester. I know him. He is just 16. I don't think he would even be in the Klan. I don't think he is old enough. But he had the hood. He shot my mother. I went to school with him. I know Stan Hester. He shot my mother. I saw him." By this time, Tannie was crying and shaking. Sheriff Richards patted her on the shoulder and took her to her seat in the courtroom, next to Arreda and the Binghams.

Tannie thought to herself, 'If he does not tell the truth, I will tell the jury what I saw.' She also knew her father had named Stan Hester as the one who shot her mother, so he must have seen him take the hood off; otherwise, how did he know it was Stan Hester? There were things that just did not add up as to why her father did not want the court to know that she saw men in Klan hoods. Maybe they *were* pillow-slips with the eye-holes cut in them.' As Tannie sat waiting for court to start, she saw Sheriff Richards talking to her father, but did not think anything about it until later.

Mrs. Stewart could not, before she died, tell police who actually shot her and not being able to pinpoint who was responsible was a problem, her testimony could not be used to prosecute anyone. Because of Alice's grave condition and the fact she was on pain medication, her testimony of identifying Pete Barber as one in the gang of men was not given credibility; it was dismissed.

Little Lorene, who was now six years old, was not allowed to testify as she was just a child given to hysteria the night her mother was killed and she might become upset if she were on the stand.

Court Begins when Reverend Robert Stewart Testifies

A death-like stillness filled the crowded courtroom when Stewart mounted the witness stand and recited in detail what happened on the night of the alleged attempt to kidnap him. When Reverend Robert Stewart stood, he was apparently cool, but had a grim set face. He was the principal witness.

"I was asleep," he said. "when my wife called to me and said that I was wanted. I dressed and went out to three automobiles in front of the house. As I drew near, I became suspicious and halted. Instantly I was seized, gagged, and forced into one of the cars. As I was seized, I screamed, and my wife rushed out with a pistol. She was begging them to let me go. Two men advanced forward as though they would seize her. It was then that she shot twice toward these men, aiming low so as to stop them, but not kill them. Another shot rang out and my wife fell. Then there was another shot fired into her back as she lay prostrate on the ground."

After reiterating the movements of each person that night, Stewart stated, "I positively identify James Hendrix and his two sons, Owen and Hubert, and Tate Gather and Pete Barber as being among the men in the gang that night."

Next Reverend Stewart, who acted as the prosecuting attorney for the state, brought up the evidence learned about Hendrix's automobile. It was sought to prove the car used on the night of the shooting was that of Hendrix; that the tracks led from the Stewart home to that of Hendrix's home. That the car identified as being tagless the night of the alleged raid had a tag on it the next morning; that the tracks made by the car on the night of November 13 were identical by comparison with tracks made by Hendrix's car.

Glynn Cook Testified for the State

Glynn Cook, a nineteen-year-old from Draketown testified, "I was walking back from Reeves' Mercantile Store on that night—the night of the attack. I had been in there to get a musterole salve for my baby sister who was sick with a cough. Mama said to go get it. That night was very cold and I was surprised to see three cars coming into town, after dark. These cars parked outside the store as I left. I was even in line with the third car when they all came to a stop. I looked at the men inside; there were about eight or nine men, and there sat James Hendrix. I looked him straight in the eyes like I'm doing right now."

Glynn Cook sat not five feet from the defendant who was sitting casually and looked, seemingly with mild interest, at the witness as he testified.

"It's the same man I saw that night. I nodded to him, but he looked away. I know James Hendrix. I've lived in Draketown all my life and so has he. I remember wondering what these three cars of men were doing out so late and on so cold a night. I had a flashlight and was in a hurry to get home. I pulled my coat up to my ears and pulled my hat down and ran home still wondering, 'What's James Hendrix doing in that car load of men?' But I didn't think anything about it until I heard about the attack the next day. That's when I went to Sheriff Richards about what I had seen. I didn't look into the other cars to see if I recognized anyone else; I just saw James Hendrix."

Gail Cook Testified for the State

Draketown resident Gail Cook, eighteen-year-old cousin of Glynn Cook who had testified before her, had requested to testify.

Outside before the trial, Gail had told Tannie, whom she knew from her Sunday School class at District Line Methodist Church, "I didn't sleep a wink last night. I kept going over and over in my head what I was going to say. I want to do this. This is my Christian duty to try my best to see that the scoundrels be punished for your mother's death. Your mother was one of the kindest persons I have ever known and was always so good to me. I still cannot believe what happened to her."

The courtroom, Haralson Co. Old Courthouse

As they walked up the stairway to the second floor, Tannie took Gail's hand and whispered so as not to be overheard, "Aren't you afraid of what the moonshiner's might do to you when you testify against them?"

Gail replied, still talking very quietly as they walked into the courtroom, "I should be, but I'm not."

Gail and Tannie stopped. Gail said, "I didn't realize there would be this many people here. My mouth is so dry, I don't know if I will be able to speak. I wish my knees would quit shaking."

As Gail neared the front of the courtroom, Robert Stewart approached her and told her to go to sit in the witness room. That meant she would be sitting in the room with witnesses for the defendant. She grew nervous.

Once in the witness room, Gail kept quiet, looking at the floor to avoid eye-contact so maybe no one would talk to her or even notice her. She pulled her coat tightly round her and pulled her hat down and sat in the closest chair to the door. Most of the witnesses packed in this little room were for the defense; they were there to say James Hendrix was innocent. She felt uncomfortable and wished her time on the stand would come soon.

Tannie sat near the front of the courtroom on the end of a row of long benches, next to Arreda and the Binghams.

In about half an hour, Robert Stewart called out, "We call Gail Cook to the stand."

Gail told later that she felt like she was in a dream. She looked over to the jury and noticed that they seemed to be mostly farmers, maybe a few store owners and there was one banker she knew. The jury looked very stern and serious. She thought, 'I wish I could walk right out the door. But I'm committed now.' She knew she was an important witness for the prosecution. When she lay her hand on the Bible and stated her name, she looked straight into the eyes of James Hendrix, who they said was the leader that night.

"Now, Miss Cook, tell the jury what you saw and heard on the morning after my wife, Alice, was shot. Just relax and tell it like you told me earlier when we were preparing for the prosecution," Robert Stewart said to the jury and the audience. He knew he was giving Miss Cook some time to collect herself as he noticed she sat like she was petrified.

Gail spoke slowly with determination, "The next morning—Friday morning, I know it was that day because I heard about what happened to Mrs. Stewart later that day when I went up to Draketown." She continued, "I was out early— about 7:00 feeding the chickens when I saw three men run out of the woods and go to the well shelter. I thought something was wrong because they looked scared and they were dirty, like they had fallen down a couple of times. They did not see me because I jumped behind the trunk of a big oak tree in the side yard—close to the chicken pen.

"They let the bucket down into the well. It took a couple minutes to fill the bucket with water at the bottom of the well, and then to get it back up. I had several minutes to watch them. It was all three of the Hendrix—the daddy, James there," she nodded toward James Hendrix, looked him straight in the eyes, "and his two sons, Owen and Hubert. They drank several dippers of the water—taking turns. They looked around toward the barn. One said, 'Let's go in and hide' but James, the daddy said, 'Let's keep moving. We can be home before long and say that we were there all night.'"

"Thanks you, Miss Cook. You did good," Robert Stewart spoke kindly to her.

The defense attorney approached her and scolded down at her like she was a bad child. He stood a little too close to her, towering over her as he was a very tall man. Then he demanded, "What time did you say you saw these three men?"

"7:00," replied a weak little voice.

"Well this was on the morning of Friday, November 14; I have the Almanac here that shows the sun doesn't come up on November 14 until 7:08. Do you see in the dark, Miss Cook?"

"No Sir, but it was already light enough to tell who they were. The Hendrix live a mile down the road from where we live and I see them passing all the time. They've lived there since I was small; I know them and I recognized them."

"Well Miss Cook, did you run tell your Daddy that three men were getting water from his well?"

"No sir." I didn't think anything about it at the time. I figured they had been on a trip and were thirsty before they reached their farm."

"Miss Cook. I think you were dreaming," the defense attorney spoke in a belittling manner, "First you said you saw three men in the dark, before daylight and then you did not tell anyone. I think you might be mistaken." He turned from her and looked at the Judge then the jury and announced. "No further questions."

Robert Stewart came back to the stand to cross examine Gail Cook.

"Miss Cook, do you feed the chickens in the dark?"

Gail faltered, confused and replied, "No Sir."

"Why not?"

"Well I suppose I would not be able to see to go down the hill to the pen and might fall on the big roots of the old trees in our yard."

Robert Stewart,"Why did you say you recognized the three men?"

Gail looked thoughtful and replied slowly. "Well, I knew it was Mr. Hendrix right away. He has worn that same light and dark, big old coat since I can remember."

Stewart, "Why do you say light and dark coat."

The young girl, "Well some of the threads are light brown and some are dark brown—it's kinda tweed. Everybody can tell when you see that coat coming that Mr. Hendrix is wearing it."

Robert Stewart turned to the judge, "I would like for exhibit A to be brought forward." The bailiff, brought a coat and handed it to Reverend Stewart.

"Now Gail, can you identify this coat?"

"Oh. That's it. That's James Hendrix coat," Gail said emphatically. "See the light and dark brown threads—the tweed, like I told you?"

"This is the one he was wearing the morning you saw him at the well shelter on your daddy's property?"

"Yes."

There was a shuffle and murmur in the courtroom when the bailiff took the coat from Stewart. Some people laughed.

"What else can you tell me about identifying these men?" Stewart asked.

"Well I knew right off it was Owen; he's kinda short and stocky and has that long hair. And there stood that long tall, skinny Hurbert with his long neck and baseball cap on—like he always wears. They were unmistakable."

"Thank you, Miss Cook. You may be excused."

With that Gail sat in the audience with the Binghams and Tannie who all shifted down and moved closer together for her to find room to sit on the bench beside them. Gail visibly let out a sigh of relief.

He called James Hendrix to the stand. He had the bailiff bring back the tweed coat to him.

Holding the coat in front of Hendrix, he asked, "Mr. Hendrix, is this your coat?" Hendrix nodded.

"Sir, speak up. Yes or no?"

" Yes it is," answered Hendrix.

"Mr. Hendrix, did you wear this coat to court yesterday and the day before?"

"No sir. I did not."

"Why?"

"Because it was tagged to be an exhibit."

Buchanan Old Courthouse courtroom

Photographs by John B. Bailey

"Do you have another coat?"

"No sir, I do not. And I've been cold for two days. Do I get my coat back today?"

Hendrix was excused. Several other witnesses were called for the prosecution.

After these witnesses, Robert Stewart paced back and forth across the courtroom in summation. Then he announced, "Your honor, that concludes my testimony and the testimonies of the witnesses. The state rests its case against James Hendrix.

It was 1:30 in the afternoon. A short break was called.

When the prosecution had ended, Tannie had not been called to testify. She realized that her father was not going to allow her to testify. When she also realized her father was not going to tell about some of the men who were in the third car, wearing hoods, she confronted him again as to why he was not telling the whole story.

He became very angry with her, and growled out, low and confidential, close to her, "I told you to leave it alone."

Tannie thought he looked almost menacing and became so upset that she left the courtroom. On her way out, Boots Bingham followed her to find out why she was leaving.

"Tannie," he was following her down the stairs to the first floor and outside. "I know you're upset. What can I do to help you?" Tannie was shaking and tears were streaking down her face. "I want to leave here. I can't take this anymore."

In minutes, Tannie and Boots were sitting on the low bench. Gail Cook followed them and sat down beside Tannie. No one spoke. They sat there watching the crowd of people, some coming out, many going in to hear the defense. Cars and horse-drawn wagons were parked everywhere.

During the break, many who were seated ate a sandwich they had brought, sitting where they were—so as not to lose their seat.

Defense Begins

The defense began and for the next three hours, some of the forty witnesses were placed on the stand, sworn in, and gave statements in favor of James Hendrix's innocence.

The spectators in the courtroom were outraged when the other four men, Owen Hendrix, Hubert Hendrix, Tate Gather and Charles "Pete" Barber, who had been arrested, detained for two months and who also faced trial for the murder of Alice Stewart, were allowed to testify and give alibis for James Hendrix and for themselves, one by one. This brought strong protest from the prosecution who stated that in as much as these men are not on trial the testimony was irrelevant.

Judge Frank A. Irvin, who was presiding, ruled that as the men were indicted jointly the testimony was permissible.

The purpose of the defense in seeking alibis for the men not on trial was for effect in case of acquittal for James Hendrix. Alibi testimony for these men was still being introduced when Judge Irvin dismissed court at 5:00, to resume the next morning at 8:00.

The defense stated it expected that testimony seeking to prove an alibi for James Hendrix would be the concluding evidence for the next day. "We expect to close by Wednesday, noon."

Buchanan Courthouse, Wednesday, February 4, 1925, 8:00 a.m.

When court resumed at 8:00 a.m., the courtroom was packed as it was the day before. Judge Irvin announced, "the cases against the other four men who were recently arrested, Ben Cash, Harry Hicksley, Emmett Hicksley, and Joe Cash will not be tried at this term of court. They are now being held in the Tallapoosa Jail."

The defense continued: "It has been established that Mrs. Stewart was shot with a bullet from a .38 pistol. I will bring it into question that Alice Stewart was shot with Reverend Robert Stewart's gun."

There was an audible, collective gasp from the audience. Those who were still a little sleepy and cold on this early, winter morning suddenly became focused to hang onto each word from the lawyers and judge.

Buchanan Old Courthouse courtroom

When the lawyer stated that the bullet which gravely wounded Alice Stewart came from the Pastor's own gun, Robert Stewart, who represented himself, told the jury and judge that this was a preposterous accusation. He reminded the judge, lawyers, and those present in the courtroom, that he had left his gun in the parsonage and Alice herself had the gun in her hand and fired it at two men who had just put him into the car where he was being bound and gagged.

Stewart, himself, was then called to be cross-examined. Robert came back with the rebuttal, "If you think these bullets match, prove it. I carry a revolver that takes a different bullet; the bullet that lodged in my wife's spine was a bullet from a .38. Though I checked my pistol in with the Sheriff at the door, I do have on my cartridge belt."

Stewart stood, pulled back the side of his suit coat to reveal that he indeed wore a cartridge belt filled with bullets around his waist. He removed one of the bullets and submitted it for comparison to the bullet which was taken out of his wife's spine, which was identified by the crime bureau as having come from a .38 revolver. The two bullets were taken to the podium for the judge and the prosecuting attorneys to compare. One of the attorneys turned to the courtroom and to Stewart and announced, "They do not match."

"Sir, they do not match because I carry a .45 revolver and wear in my cartridge belt those bullets that go into the .45." Robert thought to himself, 'this is a ploy to confuse everyone. This latest accusation is throwing the focus off the real facts.'

After the comparison of the two bullets which in no way matched, the subject was dropped.

Next the defense lawyer stated, "I shall undertake to prove that James Hendrix does not own such a gun." He called James Hendrix to the stand.

James Hendrix testified that he was at home the night of the attack at the parsonage. "Gentlemen, I come before you an innocent man. I was not in the party which killed Mrs. Stewart. I was at home with my children. I didn't hear of the killing until two days later when the sheriff came to examine my automobile and gun. I showed him my 12-gauge shotgun. I have never owned a revolver in my life."

"I was at home with my wife and my two sons, Owen and Hubert. Homer Kytle, from the dry goods store stopped by to bring some of his wife's pear preserves to my wife. He saw us all there."

Kytle was called to the stand to testify. "I was at the Hendrix home about 8:00 that night. I stopped by on my way home. My wife had asked me for several days to take this jar of pears she had made to Mrs. Hendrix. When I was there giving her the pears, I did see Mr. Hendrix at home—in the living room with his wife; his two sons were out getting stove wood to bring in that night. It was cold. I remember that. And I remember seeing all the Hendrix there at their house."

After a recess for lunch, the defense continued. James Hendrix was called back to the stand and asked several questions. He related briefly his movements the day of and the day following the killing. His testimony was followed by testimony of his two sons, Owen and Hubert. They each were called to the stand. Each testified to being at home that night. Each told about Mr. Kytle coming by and that they were there, bringing in the firewood and building a fire in the stove.

Other witnesses testified of visiting the older Hendrix's home on the fatal night and of seeing the three defendants there.

After the rebuttal testimony, which for the most part was more or less on technical points, the state closed, and arguments was begun.

Evidence in the case was concluded at 3:00 and the arguments and judge's charge consumed the next six hours. At 9:00 the case was given to the jury. After one hour of deliberation, the jury was ordered to retire for the night by Judge Irvin, but to resume for further deliberation of the case on Thursday morning at 8:00.

Thursday, February 5, 1925—Not Guilty

The fact that Reverend Stewart identified five of the men did not hold up as all had irrefutable alibis. The defense presented alibis that the accused were elsewhere the night of the shooting and to the surprise of many, the jury concluded there was insufficient evidence on which to base a guilty verdict.

The Atlanta Constitution, Thursday, February 5, 1925,
Hendrix Freed in Stewart Case

A verdict of "not guilty" was returned here this morning by the jury in the case of James Hendrix, tried in Haralson Superior Court for the murder of Mrs. Robert Stewart last November.

The verdict was rendered at 9:30, after the jury had considered the case one hour Wednesday night and one hour and 20 minutes after going to the jury room at 8:00 this morning.

Hendrix showed no emotion at the announcement of the jury's verdict, but stepped forward and eagerly shook hands with each of the jurors, who had held his life in balance. He immediately made $2,000 bond for each for his two sons, Owen and Hurbert, indicted jointly with him on the murder charge. After which, father and sons were released.

Charles "Pete" Barber and Tate Gather indicted jointly with the Hendrix were also released on $2,000 bond. Three of the four men held in Tallapoosa jail in the case have been given their liberty. They are Emmett and Harry Hicksley and Joe Cash. Ben Cash is still held.

Immediately after receiving the Hendrix verdict, Judge Irvin adjourned court; the next session to convene in August. After the bond was set and the men released, Judge Irwin refused to dismiss the indictment against the other four defendants: Hubert and Owen Hendrix, Tate Gather and Charles "Pete" Barber. It is assumed that these men would be placed on trial at the next session. Ben Cash remained in the Tallapoosa jail pending his trial, also.

Those Accused

Ben Cash, the last one arrested, paid $2,000 bond and was free until his trial.

Each of the accused went to trial at the consecutive court terms, either in January or August: Charles "Pete" Barber in August of 1925; Owen Hendrix in January of 1926; Tate Gather in August of 1926; and Hubert Hendrix in January 1927. Ben Cash went to trial in August 1927.

Witnesses appeared for the prosecution, but each time the credibility of the witness came into question or the testimony was ruled not admissible and dismissed. With the subsequent trials and disappointments of the general public and of the prosecuting attorneys, the crowds attending the trials dwindled. Each time the people came to the court trials hopeful of justice, and each time they were dismayed when the defendant went free. In turn, the accused perpetrators became more confident of freedom and began to go about their daily lives as they did "before all this trouble started." Alibis were taken as a key factor in the acquittal of each man.

A verdict of "not guilty" was returned here this morning by the jury in the case of James Hendrix, tried in Haralson Superior Court for the murder of Mrs. Robert Stewart last November.

Chapter 10
Thunderball Over Draketown

January 1989 Villa Rica Beauty Shop

Arreda came into the beauty shop all excited. "Today's story is about one of the biggest events in my life," she told Trisha. The dedication day of the memorial monument is a day I will never forget. I had never seen that many people in my life and they were all there just beyond my bedroom window. The morning of the dedication, I looked out my window to 'a sea of white'—probably 200 Ku Klux Klan members. The robed men, the Klansmen, were everywhere. These memories of this day will always be with me."

"I heard a knock on my bedroom door. My daddy opened the door, told me to get ready, and quickly straighten up my bedroom."

"'A photographer from Reese Photography Studio in Cedartown is downstairs. He wants to take photos of the day's events from your bedroom window. It seems to be a perfect vantage point from the second story,' he told me."

"In a few minutes, a man with a tall tripod came into the bedroom, moved my bed, and rearranged the furniture, rather quickly. He attached the camera so it was pointed below and beyond at the draped monument. I glanced out my other window—to the front and saw that the town was filling up with automobiles, horse-drawn wagons and buggies, some riding horseback and those on foot; people were coming from everywhere to gather around the monument."

The Ku Klux Klan Purchased the Memorial Monument

On May 31, 1925, at 11:00 a.m. in Draketown, a memorial monument was unveiled to honor the memory of the late Alice "Wildie" Adams Stewart. The Ku Klux Klan, who came forward in support, was responsible for the purchase, in charge

L-R: Dr. Hogue's office (left), livery stable, Lib Stephen's house, steeple in top background is Dr. Goldin's home. Top right corner: Oss Carroll's Store. Center: Lorene has pulled the cord to unveil the monument as about 200 Ku Klux Klan look on. Photo Courtesy Todd Slate.

of the installation, and conducted the unveiling ceremony. The Klansmen gathered at the Draketown Baptist Church grove and marched together the 1/4 mile into town to the monument. This parade was led by Solicitor Emmett Smith of Carrollton city court and Reverend H. J. Holliday of Ranburne, Alabama. The morning had started with a big song service in the school and those who had been in the singing joined the march into town at the back of the parade. More that 4,000 people, more than the entire population of Haralson County, gathered at Draketown to witness the unveiling.

A public subscription had been taken in the preceeding months to purchase and erect the monument for Mrs. Stewart; the Klansmen raised $80. The monument committee was composed of Mrs. W. L. Meek, chairman, Mrs. W. L. Hogue, Mrs. J. E. Wood, Mrs. Guy Poole, Miss Callie Allgood and T. W. Hembree. It was under the direction of the committee that the funds were raised and the money was turned over to the Ku Klux Klan for the monument to be erected.

The Ku Klux Klan had purchased a memorial monument made of pure, white

Georgia marble, had it inscribed, and placed it at the site where Alice Stewart was murdered. They placed it adjacent and within three feet—out of the road—to where she fell mortally wounded.

When the speakers moved to the raised platform in front of the crowd, a

May 31, 1925 Monument Dedication. Speakers on left facing crowd. Lorene in left foreground facing monument (dark hat and dress). Dr. Hogue's office in the background. (The News-Herald, Franklin, Pennsylvania 6/6/1925)

silence akin to reverence affected the gathering crowd and when the hour of unveiling arrived—11:00—as if by magic, the buzz of undertone conversation ceased. Mrs. Jesse Hogue, a member of the local monument committee, delivered the invocation. Reverend J. C. Moody made a few remarks on the purpose of the occasion.

The introduction was made by Reverend Robert Stewart: "I would like to thank each and everyone of you for being here today. A year-and-a-half ago, I brought my family to Draketown thinking that we could help the good people of this good community. We were welcomed with open arms and open hearts. We are in the middle of a struggle between the law of the land, the laws of prohibition and the laws of our maker and Savior, and the lawlessness of alcohol and greed."

"We meet here today to dedicate this monument to my dear wife, and mother of my children, who gave her life trying to protect me. Let this monument to her be a reminder for us to continue the battle for a better life for all people. Let this monument remind us to give thanks for each day we have on this earth. We never know if it will be our last." Stewart sat down, wiping his eyes with a handkerchief fetched from his back pocket.

All the speakers were eulogistic of Mrs. Alice Stewart and spoke in glowing terms of her heroism and martyrdom to the cause of law and order. The general tone of the addresses were against lawlessness and particularly the crime of "rum running," it being claimed that the Stewart trouble was caused by the relentless fight made by Reverend Stewart, both personally and in the pulpit, against whisky making and selling.

Dr. Elam F. Dempsey, secretary of education for the North Georgia Methodist Conference in Atlanta, made the principal unveiling address. Dr. Dempsey paid tribute to Alice Stewart's martyred death.

May 31, 1925, view of the parsonage from the north side of the monument
The Atlanta Constitution 6/4/25

He said, "Martyr blood is never shed in vain. It is the seed from which—ever springs a harvest of heroism and of good. Mrs. Robert Stewart, brave martyr, to love, duty, and law enforcement is too lofty a spirit to be adequately memorialized by any material monument. Bronze, granite and marble have no tongues eloquent enough to perpetuate the name and message of this martyr-heroine of the parsonage. Gold and silver and precious stones shrink into the commonplace when they endeavor to memorialize her. Her heroic spirit was indeed a candle of the Lord lighted from the flame of His infinite love and wisdom. Its fitting memorial must therefore be spiritual in its nature. The example of the faithful daily life reaching its climax in her heroic death is a flame to kindle like fidelity and heroism in countless thousands of other kindred spirits. Humanity blesses (illegible) when it enshrines in its memory such a woman as Mrs. Robert Stewart, willing martyr to holy love."

Dr. C. W. Downy of Tallapoosa echoed the feeling of the crowd: "This monument will ensure that Alice Wildie Adams Stewart will always be remembered through the ages for her love, her bravery, and her sacrifice. She gave her life trying to protect her husband."

"We have a *'Stolen Life—A Promise Made'*: her life was stolen from her; this monument represents a promise made that she will not be forgotten."

Lorene Stewart, the six-year-old daughter of Mrs. Stewart, assisted by Mrs. W. L. Meek and her granddaughter, Ella Ruth McClendon pulled the cords that loosed the draperies over the monument. They fell away to reveal a shaft of white; a marble obelisk monument with a thunderball sphere at the top towering fifteen feet above the crowd.

A small oval black-and-white porcelain photograph of Alice Stewart was embedded on one side of the monument n the center above the inscription:

Lorene, Ms. Meeks, Ella McClendon
The Atlanta Journal, June 1, 1925
Courtesy, Kathy Rechsteine

ALICE WILDIE ADAMS
WIFE OF
REV. ROBERT STEWART
BORN MAY 10, 1888
ASSASSINATED NOV 13, BY THE RUM
RUNNERS AT THIS PLACE
AND DIED AT WESLEY MEMORIAL
HOSPITAL NOV 15, 1924
SHE WAS A KIND AND AFFECTIONATE WIFE
A FOND MOTHER AND FRIEND TO ALL

Look not thou upon the wine when it is
red, when it giveth his colour in the cup
when it moveth itself aright.
At the last it biteth like a serpent and
stingeth like an adder.
My fruit is better than gold, yea than
fine gold and my revenue than choice silver.

Open Air Meeting

After the monument dedication, there was an open air meeting at the Draketown Baptist Church grove led by Solicitor Smith and Reverend Mr. Holliday. Their Klansmen's hoods were thrown back over their robes, and they stood on an improvised platform—the back of a wagon. Solicitor Smith asserted that the Klan stood for law and order and appealed to all other Haralson county citizens for respect for law and order and for assistance in apprehending Mrs. Stewart's slayers.

"As members of the Knights of the Invisible Empire, our undertaking is a serious one. We must be positive doers, not negative professors. We call for the sanctity of laws and promotion of respect for law and order. Let me say this—we believe the mere fact that we have come here today, to take part in this ceremony, speaks louder than any words."

Reverend Mr. Holliday spoke condemning the man who takes a "little dram," who keeps a little in his house, who carries a little in his pocket—in fact "anyone who is not law abiding."

After the Open Air Meeting adjourned, over half the people left town; the others—hundreds—moved to a shaded area under a grove of trees near the church where a big basket dinner was spread. Each family had a picnic basket or hamper or bag brimming over with more than enough to feed not only their family, but they had prepared extra for the public who had come to the unveiling ceremony. The ladies had prepared for those who had traveled a distance to be there this day; people came from all over the county and as far away as Atlanta.

Under one-hundred-year-old oak trees were long lines of plank tables, many added this last week by both the Methodist and Baptist men from churches in the area who worked to make this day a success. Some families brought portable tables and folding chairs that were set up under the shade of these trees. But most families spread a blanket or old table cloth on the ground and sat on the edges. This picnic spread from the road all the way down to the spring, all the way to the church on the left and even down toward the school on the right. The blankets and cloths were so close that you could hardly walk between them.

As the people lined up to serve their plate, a blessing was offered by the Baptist pastor, A. J. Garner. His orator-type voice projected over the crowd, "Lord bless this food for the nourishment of our bodies and we pray that each and every one here today will have a safe journey home."

It was a beautiful warm early summer day and the picnic was ready: the spread of food on the long tables included sliced ham, fried chicken, homemade bread, hard boiled eggs, tea cakes, and fried pies; the men of the community had vast amounts of lemonade made from cool, clear spring water.

Melviney, Jackson, Boots, and Bud were in the process of getting their food, then sitting down on the blanket Jackson had spread. Omega and Alpha had attended the unveiling ceremony then walked slowly to the grove where folding chairs and a card table were set for them. Omega said there were too many bugs at a picnic for her.

Lorene sat beside Arreda and ate with the Binghams. Tannie and Boots sat together away from the others. Robert Stewart stayed with the dignitaries from Atlanta.

Melviney looked around at all the people and then at all the food, wondering if there would be enough for everyone to have a small portion. At the end of the meal, there was food left!

She commented to those around her sitting on the blanket, "This is like when Jesus fed the multitudes of people with just 5 loaves of bread and 2 fishes. No one in their wildest dreams would have thought this many people would show up today."

Tannie told Boots, "I just want people to stop telling me how sorry they are about my mother. Hundreds have said that to me. It doesn't make it any easier."

"Well, they are just trying to make you feel better. That's all they know how to do," Boots smiled at her. "Here, have a tea cake." He put the cookie on her plate.

She smiled back. "Well I guess they do mean well. But I wish it would all just go away. I do feel better when you're around." She touched him on the arm, then munched on the tea cake, smiling at him again.

Any other time when a crowd of people got together, the kids would be running and playing; someone would be playing a fiddle or guitar; there would be laughing, talking, and funny tales. But today the people were solemn and sad and after the meal, stood in

Photo by Trisha Mullinax, 1990

small groups talking among themselves about the trial last February and the upcoming trial in August.

Someone said, "I wonder if justice will ever be done for Alice Stewart?" Some shook their head in a show of disbelief of those at liberty—out on bond awaiting trial.

In the days to come, all 4,000 plus people who had attended the unveiling ceremony would never forget—the crowd, the monument, and the speakers, and those who stayed, remembered the picnic for a lifetime. Many continued to pray for the pastor and his daughters and that justice would be done for Alice Stewart.

Summer Vacation

The next day after the unveiling was Monday, June 1, 1925, and school was out. It was summer. Arreda walked down the street from her house to look closer at the monument. Buster followed along beside her. She was still thinking about the day as she had never seen so many people in one place in her life.

As Arreda approached the monument, she noticed Lorene sitting on one of the marble benches that was part of the monument. She waved to her; Lorene waved back. Arreda quietly sat on the bench to the left side. "You did a good job yesterday. Were you scared?"

"Nah," Lorene replied, swinging her feet as her legs dangled above the ground. She looked sad. "No, I wasn't scared. I was sad. About my mother." She sighed and looked to the side of the shaft to the small photograph embedded in the monument.

"I miss her. I was also excited about seeing the monument," she explained.

The two girls left the benches. They ran around and around the monument, laughing. Buster barked at them as they ran and laughed.

"It sure is tall," said Arreda looking upward as she ran. They were both looking up at the thunderball sphere on the top and looking at the background—the clear, blue June sky.

"Daddy says up there is where Mother lives, now," she pointed to the sky, "in heaven."

"Martyr blood is never shed in vain. It is the seed from which ever springs a harvest of heroism and of good."
Dr. Elam F. Dempsey

Chapter 11
Moonshiners Without a Still

June 10, 1925

Ten days after the unveiling ceremony and nine days after Arreda and Lorene talked and ran around the monument in Draketown, Robert Stewart married Miss Mattie Woods in Paulding County.

Reverend Robert Stewart, who was affectionately called by his congregation, Preacher Bob, set about to select a mother for his daughters and a wife for himself. He let the girls decide. They picked from two possible choices. His daughters knew the two ladies from church where their Daddy was an itinerate pastor. They were given a choice, Mattie Wood or another lady. Tannie picked Mattie Wood and Lorene agreed; obviously, Mattie was Preacher Bob's first choice.

Later, family members would describe Stewart as a wanderlust always up for travel and adventure. He was an ambitious man and always kept busy. At every parsonage he lived in, he *had* to build a storm shelter. Mattie was known for her strict religious discipline even more so than the pastor.

One Sunday afternoon, as they sat on the front porch, he said suddenly, "Let's ride over to see the new bridge that's been built; that ought to be fun."

Mattie reminded him sternly, "No we can't do that. Remember, it's Sunday. Riding over to see a bridge is not keeping the Sabbath day holy." They stayed home that Sunday.

Toby Howard and Family

Toby Howard was unable to continue working the Hendrix still. His uncle and two cousins were on trial, the sessions of which stretched out over two years. After James Hendrix was released on bond, he felt as if he were being watched. During the two months the Hendrix were in jail, the time they were in court, and the time they were out on bond, they never contacted Toby. They knew if they were to continue making moonshine, they would have to do it elsewhere. James Hendrix was the first to leave town. His plans were after each of his two sons Hubert and Owen were tried, if each of them were acquitted as he had been, they would join him in another county where they were all unknown.

Toby also felt that he was being watched. He did not visit his Hendrix kin in jail; he was not part of the crowd at the court trials and he did not go to their house after they were acquitted. Each knew any contact could be incriminating for him.

None of them ever visited the still again after the arrests. It was left the way it was on the night Toby was walking home through the woods and heard the hounds howling and the car brakes squeal on the road ahead of him. This was the early morning when he had run home and was visited right after daybreak by the sheriff and posse when he left his muddy wet clothes and shoes in the kitchen. He realized later that they had seen his pile of clothes on the floor. Having wet clothes and wet shoes in the early morning meant they had not been laying there all night, that he had just come in and was pretending to have slept at home all night. He knew the sheriff was suspicious.

Toby and his wife, Mollie, had to manage, somehow, without the income from the still. They lived off what food she had canned and dried that past summer. Mollie had to feed herself, her husband, and their six children with no income until next spring's garden produced enough vegetables for them. She took as little as she dared of the money in the fruit jar buried in the corner of the barn so it would last all winter to help supplement their meals.

When spring came, Toby planted corn and soybeans like a typical farmer. He went 1/4's for corn and 1/3's for soybeans with the owner of the tenant house and land where they lived. His older boys dropped out of school to help him farm.

Clyde Barber, Telma, Janice, Johnny and Junior

After Tom and Pete Barber were arrested, the liquor making in their family came to a halt. With no moonshine to transport, Clyde's trippin' into Atlanta stopped. While his cousin, Pete, was in jail and out on bond waiting for his trial all summer, the sheriff and posse seemed to be everywhere. Clyde could not safely contacted Pete, even if he wanted to.

Clyde saved enough money to pay Merilou until March when Junior would be two years old, old enough to eat soft food from the table and wean him from nursing to drink from a cup. He also had saved enough to budget through the winter months without income.

In the early spring, Clyde took one last trip to Buchanan in his older truck. He removed all the modifications from his truck so it was as he had bought it. He drove to Buchanan Tractor Company and traded his truck for a tractor—even trade. He had to wait most of the day, but the men there delivered the tractor on a large flat bed truck, also giving him a ride home now since he did not own a vehicle.

The next day, he took the tractor over the hill, cut off the motor, and stood beside it. He surveyed the land as far as he could see and scooped down, grabbed a double handful of red Georgia soil, and held it in his hands, turning it and studying it. He dropped it and continued to survey his land.

He thought back, 'I'm the third generation trying to make something out of this soil. Back when it was a plantation, there were hands to work and produce. After the war, everything fell economically. His Dad literally walked away from it. Now here he was with a modern tractor. A morning dove cooed from the line of woods beyond the fields—a sure sign of rain. He wondered, 'Was this an omen that he could, with the tractor, produce enough to care for his family without doing anything illegal ever again?'

Clyde plowed his eighty acres, half for corn and half for peas. He would pay help, if need be, in produce at harvest time. He would also hire out—plow for other farmers. If the farmer could not pay a fee for the service of plowing their fields, he would take barter—chickens, eggs, smoked hog meat, greens, anything.

Charles "Pete" Barber on Trial August 1925

When Tom had been let go because of his alibi of having a neck injury because of the mule's harness around his neck, Pete became confident that he would be acquitted. Pete's alibi came from Homer Kytle, a man whom he supplied with whisky anytime he wanted it, often and plenty. Mr. Kytle, the manager at a feed store near Buchanan, appeared as a witness for Pete and told the jury how he had sent Pete into Atlanta in his company truck to pick up a load of chicken feed.

"Pete left in the afternoon. He got back about 6:00. I was in the store in Buchanan when he unloaded all those bags. It probably took him an hour to unload it, stack it in the store room, and sweep up. There was no way he could have been in Draketown that night."

Mr. Kytle had the receipt from his Atlanta supplier. At the bottom of the receipt is where Pete had initialed P. B. enough to vouch for his signature. Pete then wrote his initials for the court without seeing the paper Mr. Kytle held. When the initials matched, that won the jury over. The judge and jury did not know that Mr. Kytle visited Pete before he went to trial and Pete signed the blank receipt then. In truth, the driver who picked up the chicken feed in Atlanta had not signed the receipt at all.

After Pete's acquittal, he was happy, cocky, and eager to begin moonshining again. He and Tom found an ideal place on the side of Frog Creek further into the hills than they had ever gone. They came brazenly by Clyde Barber's driving too fast, waving and having a celebration, drinking, and shouting "we both 'beat that wrap.'"

They invited Clyde to join them at the new still as they needed a third man.

Clyde declined. "I figure I can make it without getting back to trippin.' It's tempting; I know how it feels to make that easy money, but the sheriff and posse and all the towns people are watching everything that goes on, especially with those who were originally arrested after the Stewart attack. I want no part of this anymore. I'm getting out of the trippin' business."

Tom and Pete convinced a neighbor to join them at their still. Two months later on an October night, they were caught. At 3:00 a.m. the revenuers who had been tracking their every move came out of the woods and surprised them. They had no chance to run. They were caught red-handed, right on the spot. Tom was stirring; Pete was testing the first drips, and the neighbor was just standing, looking confused when this gang of revenuers surrounded them. Tom did not even try to charm his way out of this. Pete could not think of anything to laugh about and the neighbor wished he had never heard of a moonshine still or of Tom and Pete Barber.

These three were tried by a federal judge, convicted, and sent to the Atlanta Penitentiary for five years.

August 14, 1925 The Atlanta Constitution, Night-Riders Flog Pastor Near Scene of Stewart Killing

Tallapoosa, Ga., August 13. The second depredation by night riders, an event closely paralleling the attack on Reverend Robert Stewart at Draketown last November which resulted in the death of the minister's wife, was reported to Sheriff Richards

Thursday morning by Reverend Henry Holmes, a Baptist minister who says he was called from the house at which he was stopping Wednesday night and roughly attacked by eight or ten men.

Reverend Holmes had been engaged in a revival meeting at Tallapoosa East church, about four miles from Buchanan this week and during his sermons he has made vigorous attacks against bootleggers, whisky runners, home wreckers and distillers.

Wednesday night he says he was called from the home of Asberry Cook, who lives in the Flatwoods section. When he went to the road where two cars had stopped he was attacked by a party of men and severely beaten by them, the men trying to force him into one of the two cars which had stopped in front of his house.

After a desperate resistance the minister succeeded in escaping from the party of men and hurried to Buchanan and placed himself under the protection of Sheriff G. B. Richards. He was suffering severely Thursday from his hurts received at the hands of his assailants.

Sheriff Richards and his entire field force have been called into activity by the second attack on a minister in this county by supposed violators of the law and every effort will be made to apprehend the men who made the attack on the minister.

Reverend Bob Continues to Raid

In his zeal against liquor manufacturers and even after his wife had been killed the year before, Robert Stewart continued to battle moonshiners. Stewart, along with W. F. McLendon, of Rockmart, Bob Austin and Green Barrett, of Rockmart, did the work of live fearless officers when on the Simpson place, some three miles from Rockmart, they took possession of a still, 1,200 gallons of still beer, ten gallons of whisky, and arrested Barney Tate and Joe Johnsson.

Stewart said, "This was not a case of

Mattie Stewart with Lorene
Courtesy Hazel Barnes

waiting until the operator left—they 'bearded the tiger in his den' and brought him out as well as his goods. That's the kind of work that counts."

In November of 1925, the family, with the new mother, was transferred to the Green County Circuit District south of Athens, Georgia in Greene County.

The new congregation joined in the fight. The publication of the pamphlet *Alcohol: A Deadly Necrotic* by G. P. Lamar expressed the sentiments of many of this time of prohibition when war was waged against liquor.

Mr. G. P. Lamar, who wrote from the heart, suffered as a child because of the effect of alcohol. His father, an alcoholic, had abandon his wife and their four children. Living in Atlanta and being unable to care for them, he began to drink. When he was out of control, he took his wife, two sons, and two daughters to Haralson County to live with her widowed mother. The family later said that in those years, they almost starved to death. George, now an adult, had hated alcohol all his life because he lived through, first hand, the hardships it had caused his family by having no father to provide for them.

Alcohol—A Deadly Necrotic
by G. P. Lamar

In times past many important men have let alcohol drag them down in disgrace. They needed alcohol as a crutch for each day. What has life become for people when they can bear it only if they are fortified by alcohol?

Why are they slaves to alcohol? It damages their brain, liver and heart. Centuries before Christ was born, Solomon described some of the effects of alcohol. "At last it biteth like a serpent and stingeth like an adder." (Proverbs 23:32) It kills and maims. I declare all out WAR on this deadly enemy. People think alcohol will make them forget their problems, but it only makes them worse.

Actually, this is a spiritual problem. This is what happens when human beings try to forget the God who made them. God is the source of our life. They think it will help them cope with life, but they will only be led to a sinner's grave and devil's hell.

January 9, 1926 The Gaffney Ledger; Greensboro, Georgia

The Raiding Parson of Draketown," who always packs a shooting iron, even to the pulpit in his lifelong hunt for the slayer of his wife in 1924, became a Green County police officer. His career as a policeman was brief—it lasted only three hours. He was appointed to the job in the morning and in the afternoon, he was fired.

He came to Green County in November of 1925, one year after Alice's death, as pastor of the Green County Circuit. At the last Conference of the North Georgia Assembly, Reverend Stewart was not given a charge and since that time he has been seeking something to do. The Green County Commissioners, in their monthly meeting Wednesday, discharged Officer T. Griffin Williams and at the same time appointed Dr. Stewart.

The news of this action spread over the town in a flash. When the County Commissioners convened for their afternoon session, a committee of Greensboro citizens waited to speak in behalf of Policeman Williams.

The upshot of the whole was that so many people opposed the discharge of Policeman Williams that the County Commissioners agreed to reinstate him. This left Dr. Stewart yet unemployed.

Stewart had not been given another assignment by the North Georgia Methodist Conference. What would he do now?

In times past many important men have let alcohol drag them down in disgrace. They needed alcohol as a crutch for each day. What has life become for people when they can bear it only if they are fortified by alcohol?

Chapter 12
A Silent Movie—The Raiding Pastor

January 1989 The Beauty Shop, Villa Rica

One winter day when Arreda continued her story, she told Trisha, "The most astounding thing happened. There was a movie about Alice Stewart. Well, it was so long ago that it was a silent movie. All the countryside was astir. They even used local actors—people from Tallapoosa. My cousin, Chesley Denman, was an actor in the movie. He told me all about how it was made."

After the pastor and his new wife, Mattie, and his daughters were transferred to Green County, Reverend Robert could not rest. He brought his family back to live in Paulding County, adjacent to Haralson County. In 1926 when Reverend Robert Stewart's campaign against liquor continued, his idea was to tell the entire story as a movie.

When Tannie heard her daddy on the phone setting the plans into motion, she confronted him. "I can't believe you are going to make a movie about my mother's death. That means someone will have to write it, people will have to act it out, and the population will be invited to see how she died." Tannie was so angry she was shaking as she spoke.

Robert Stewart had a comeback. "People need to know the situation and how we've battled the evils of alcohol to see these evils take the life of our dear wife and mother. The proceeds will go toward fighting against the making, selling, and distribution of these spirits made by those under Satan's influence."

"Well I'll not be around to hear any part of this. I'm going to my Granny Adams."

"Tannie, I can't understand why you don't want to be a part of making this movie."

"That's because I live it over and over and over every day—seeing my mother shot. I have to go on living, and I can't have a life constantly filled with sorrow with people talking about it and acting out what happened. I don't care what you say. I'm leaving."

Robert Stewart could have made his daughter stay, but thought it would be less on both of them if she did go to her Grandmother Adams.

Tannie called Reeves' store and got someone to tell Boots Bingham to call her. Because the Bingham's did not have a phone, someone would have to walk down to get Boots to come to the store and call her.

In a few hours, Boots called, listened to Tannie, and they made plans for him to drive her to Buchanan to catch the train. She called someone who lived near her grandmother in north Georgia who had a phone, to go tell her grandmother that she would be up in a few days.

Tannie was eighteen, old enough to travel alone. Boots was seventeen, old enough to borrow a car and drive Tannie to the station. Boots was a good friend, one she could call on when she needed help. In a few day, she mounted the train steps, hugged Boots good-bye, and was on her way to north Georgia and literally "out of the picture."

With more peace and quite in their little house in Paulding County, Robert Stewart set about making a motion picture. First, the Milo Moving Picture Company was formed when fifteen men from Tallapoosa came together under his leadership to make the movie **Draketown Tragedy**, later promoted as **The Raiding Parson**. Officers in the Milo Moving Picture Company were: C. W. Downey, President; F. L. Wycoff, Vice-President; R. C. Greene, Secretary; J. W. Mozley treasurer; and M. V. Sewell Financial Director.

We the undersigned, having organized ourselves together for the purpose of financing a Moving Picture to be known as the **DRAKETOWN TRAGEDY**, and the organization to be known as the **MILO MOTION PICTURE COMPANY**, therefore it is agreed:

1st: It is known and agreed, that the scenario, films, negatives and prints and all property that is now in the possession of the Company, or any member of this Company, or any property or fixture pertaining to this picture or its development is and shall be the property of the Company and not that of an individual.

2nd: That although as herein later provided that the Reverend Robert Stewart shall receive fifty percent of the net proceeds, his voting power shall be equal to one vote and not empowered with any more authority than any individual member, and that a majority of all members shall rule in any and all transactions. It is also agreed by all that a majority of eight members, which shall constitute a quorum in the absence of other member, shall be binding upon the members absent from the meeting. Provided that all members shall have been notified. Registered mail being sufficient evidence of notice to members.

3rd: It is further agreed that no member shall transact any business without the consent of a majority of the membership of this organization. And that all business and production of, or the purchasing of any material of any nature whatsoever, shall be first approved by the Company and that everything pertaining to the production of this or any other picture shall in its entirety belong to, and be the property of the Company, and cannot be disposed of in any manner without purchaser signing this agreement.

4th: It is also agreed that we will submit any and all differences that may arise between any member or members to the Company as a whole, and that a majority vote of this company shall be binding. And it is further agreed that by any and all members that before any suit for recovery of any property or possessions of any nature or privileges whatsoever, that his interest in the Company shall be forfeited, and each hereby waive all claims to suits and freely and willingly agree that a majority shall have full power and control and that any and all actions taken by a majority of the members of this Company shall be binding without (illegible).

5th: It is agreed that Reverend Robert Stewart shall have fifty per cent of the net earnings and that he shall provide fifty per cent of the expense in production of this picture. The picture always remaining, until satisfactorily sold or otherwise disposed of, the property of the Milo Motion Picture Company.

6th: In case of death of any member—His Administrator or Executor shall be possessed of the same power in this Company as the original member.

7th: No officer or member of the Company shall have the right to transact any business of any nature without the consent and approval of the Company.

8th: The executive committee shall obtain from each person taking a part in this picture a receipt for his or her services. The receipt taken specifically specifying permission to use the picture as produced without suit.

J. R. Roberts	M. V. Sewell
R. J. Miller	W. S. Mosley
J. B. Smith	W. H. Brooks
Robt. Stewart	H. Y. Hutcheson
A. E. Milvany	H. B. Walton
R. J. Carnes	F. L. Wycoff

C. W. Downey	R. C. Greene
H. F. Senft	B. A. Mobley

Signatures of members of the Milo Motion Picture Company, Courtesy Joe Mosley

The Filmmakers

Floyd Traynham (Tranham), of Winn Studio in Atlanta, wrote the story and scenes for the movie by being strongly coached by Robert Stewart. Traynham and his Winn Studio were the producers and totally responsible for the making of *Draketown Tragedy*. Randal Julian Carnes, a local short story technician, was the director who was responsible for bringing the story to life on film. The production of the movie began in the spring of 1926, the largest undertaken for a single production ever made by Winn Studios. The film involved three locations and more actors than had been used in the history of this company. The film filled six reels; seventeen copies were made.

> Milo Motion Picture Company
> Order on Treasurer
>
> Tallapoosa, Ga. July 6, 1926.
>
> Due Mrs. R. J. Carnes, for
> Playing part, 2 days.......................... $5.00
> ~~For dress—ruined in falls........................ 10.00~~
> For Make-up bought from Waldrop's for
> Resurrection Scene....................... 1.50
> $16.50
> 6.50
>
> Approved: *R. J. Carnes*
>
> *Paid, amt $6.50*
> *signed Mrs. R. J. Carnes*

Milo Motion Picture Company
Order on Treasurer

Tallapoosa, Ga. July 6, 1926.

Due Mrs. R. J. Carnes, for
    Playing part, 2 days $ 5.00
    **For dress—ruined in falls   (10.00)
    For Make-up bought from Waldrop's for
    Resurrection Scene   1.50
                                         ($16.50)
                                         $6.50

Approved: R. J. Carnes
    Paid amount $6.50
    signed Mrs. R. J. Carnes
    ** Note for dress ruined in falls was marked through and not paid.

Hamilton—Beach Film Company:

Hamilton Beach Film Company was paid $392.15 on May 25, 1926 and $313.80 on June 23, 1926 for negatives developed, negative titles, title cards, positive prints, 11 metal reels and for operator services of cutting and assembling for screening the picture.

6/23/26

Milo Motion Picture Company
Tallapoosa, Ga.

IN ACCOUNT WITH

HAMILTON-BEACH FILM CO.
PHOTOGRAPHIC LABORATORY
97 WALTON STREET,   ATLANTA GEORGIA

1600	ft. negative developed	@ .01 ft	16.00
172	ft. negative titles	@ .05	8.60
23	Title cards	@ .50	11.50
5454	ft. print	@ .05	272.70
6	metal reels	@ .50	3.00
	Operator's services for screening picture		2.00
			$ 313.80

Received check in
payment of above 6/26/26

Hamilton Beach
Film Co.
By James Hamilton

Many of the Actors were Local

Parts in the movie were played by several dozen local people from Tallapoosa: Ben Smith, Chief of Police; Brewer Murphy; Dr. C. W. Downey; Evelyn Kytle; Miss Mattie Lee Cole; Hubert Walton; W. H. Brocks; Mrs. E. S. Kytle; Waler Chapman; Chesley Denman; Mrs. Mattie New; Clifton Allen and many others. The part of Mrs. Alice Stewart was played in a highly credible manner by Mrs. Dovie Carnes, wife of the motion picture director, Randal Julian Carnes.

```
                              DATE    6/23/26  192

M    Milo Motion Picture Company

          Tallapoosa, Ga.
              IN ACCOUNT WITH
         HAMILTON - BEACH FILM CO.
            PHOTOGRAPHIC LABORATORY
97 WALTON STREET,                    ATLANTA, GEORGIA
```

1600	ft. negative developed	@ 1¢ ft.	16.00
172	ft. negative titles	@ 5¢	8.60
23	Title cards	@ 50¢	11.50
5454	ft. print	@ 5¢	272.70
6	metal reels	@ 50¢	3.00
	Operator's services for screening picture		2.00
			$313.80

Received check in payment of above 6/26/26 Hamilton Beach Film Co By James Hamilton

Scenes from the Movie

Scenes from the movie: Robert Stewart played himself and with the help of actors, re-enacted the destroying of stills typical of those he took out while he was a pastor in Draketown. The death of Alice Stewart was re-enacted in front of the parsonage. There was a recreation of the unveiling of the monument, erected on the spot where she was shot. Lorene, now seven-years-old, played herself in the unveiling of the monument scene with a smaller group of the Klan than had been at the actual unveiling ceremony the year before. Being a part of the crowd gathered to view the unveiling ceremony were members of the temperance societies of the North Georgia conference.

Copyright

W L M -

 The copyright on the picture has been printed and is ready to be sent to Washington. You will remember that the Company agreed to pay me $25 for same. If you can give me a check, dated ahead, to cover it, I will appreciate it as I am absolutely without any money due to my having lost so much time in Atlanta.

R J C

 On July 31, 1926, a check was made to R. J. Carnes for copyright to the Library of Congress.

Publicity and Advertisements

 Advertised as: Producers of the Record-Breaking Picture: "***The Raiding Parson***," a dramatic, stirring, appealing six-reel feature a story of pathos, tragedy, humor, love and adventure in the hills of North Georgia. His movie was released in 1926 with 50% of the profit going to Reverend Stewart to help in his crusade again liquor usage. He used the tragedy of his wife's death as a catalytic instrument in getting attention to his cause."

   Dallas, Ga   **6/1926**
   Mr. Mozley:

Dear Sir: Yours of the fifth to hand to day. Just back from a trip to Atlanta. Sorry about getting your letter to late about Negro Mac. I bought a $400 projecting Mac in Atlanta today.

 I feel that it (is) the only way to make a success of our picture. Put it on in as many theaters as we can. And then fill out the time in churches, school houses and auditoriums. Now Brother Mosley you know when we show in school or church houses, unless we give a % to some good cause, we must pay Lic(ense?). Now this is what I want to do to get by with this. Let a % go to the monument in

Draketown. If this will be alright with the Klan and Company.

I find that most of the theater managers are loaded down with dates. So most of our dates will be in auditoriums put on by the Klan or some other organization, some churches and school houses.

Now as I have my own Mac I would like to show our picture at Draketown if we can arrange for the Klan from Tallapoosa to be there. Also at Buchanan. I think it will make a hit at these two places. My dates at Dallas has been called off at Dallas for this week.

Certainly I will furnish you a contract before each show. Also making a settlement for each night the picture is shown.

There (are) several things I would like to mention but I haven't the time. As I must go in the other fellow's car. Haven't been able to get me one. If I had one I could (go) so much better.

Yours as ever,
Robert Stewart

Newspapers Describes the Showings of the Movie
May 27, 1926, Stewart Tragedy Put on Screen by Local People,The Atlanta Constitution, reported:

The initial presentation of the show here on Wednesday was witnessed by upwards of 2,000 people.

June 29, 1929, The Atlanta Constitution, reported:

The Raiding Parson *shows to crowd at Atlanta Municipal Auditorium on June 28, 1926. Date of the next showing in Atlanta will be announce later when all arrangements have been completed. The showing Monday night was the first here since the completion of the picture two weeks ago (about June 15, 1926.) It will be taken to towns throughout the country, where bookings have already been made.*

August 27 1926, Anniston Boy Takes Part in Murder Film, The Anniston Star page 8.
"Draketown Tragedy" *Is Shown In Picture With Many Tallapoosa People Taking Parts.*

"More than 1,000 people gathered in Anniston, Alabama at the local picture house on Wednesday evening to witness the screen production of Randal Julian

Carnes' ***The Raiding Parson***. *This movie is the picture version of the brutal murder of Mrs. Wildie Stewart of Draketown, Georgia, which occurred in front of her home on the night of November 13, 1924.*

An announcement was made following the first three shows that the picture would have a continuous run on Friday and probably later in the year. Few pictures shown here in recent years have attracted more general attention.

Announcement was made on Thursday morning that a tour which will include Anniston, Birmingham, and other Alabama cities would be started in the near future, wide publicity having been given the picture by supporters of the present prohibition laws."

Schedule of "Exhibitions" of Draketown Tragedy in 1926

May 26th - Amuzu Theatre in Tallapoosa; May 29th, afternoon and night showing.

June 7th - Sparta, Georgia

June 8th - Greensboro, Georgia

June 9th - Sparta, Georgia

June 10th & June 11th - Douglasville, Georgia

July 15th - Tallapoosa

July 27th - Alabama schedule.

Miscellaia:

On May 26, 1926, when the Amuzu Theatre in Tallapoosa showed *The Raiding Parson*, admission was 10 cents for kids and 25 cents for adults.

The actors were paid from $3.00 - $5.00 per day.

There were 6,750 circulars printed to advertise this motion picture.

On June 4, 1926, J. S. Reese's Photography Studio, in Cedartown, was paid $6.00 for one dozen photos of the re-enactment scene of the Unveiling Ceremony.

Liquidation of Milo Motion Picture Company

The Milo Motion Picture Company was liquidated in August 1926. None of the seventeen copies of the movie were returned after the liquidation.

C. W. Downey	**F. L. Wycoff**	**R. C. Green**
President	**Vice President**	**Secretary**

THE MILO MOTION PICTURE COMPANY
49 Head Avenue
Tallapoosa, Georgia
Producers and Distributors

August 13, 1926

Dear Sir:

It was decided at the last meeting of the stockholders of the Milo Motion Picture Company to begin liquidating the indebtedness of the company, as some of it is past due and some more will mature soon or to be exact September 1st.

On July 16th last one note (Mtg) for amount of $318.80 was due and another for the amount of $150.00 will be due Sep. 1st. So we have decided to liquidate it by monthly assessments this being the consensus of opinion of the stockholders themselves as the best way to go at it, at a meeting called Aug. 2, 1926.

Each member is expected to pay the amount of $25.00 on the first day of each month beginning Sept. 1st 1926 as this plan will not make it so hard on any one as it would to have to raise the entire amount at one time.

Please make your plans to meet this at this time so that it will not be so hard on any one or any number of the stockholders.

    Respectfully,
    Signed:
    W. L. Mosley - Treasurer
    M. V. Sewell - Financial Director

Copies To:
    B. A. Murphy
    R. J. Carnes
    J. B. Smith
    H. B. Walton
    W. H. Brooks
    J. R. Roberts
    H. Y. Hutcheson
    R. C. Greene
    R. Miller

F. L. Wycoff
C. W. Downey
M. V. Sewell
File

Record-Breaking Picture: "The Raiding Parson," a dramatic, stirring, appealing six-reel feature story of pathos, tragedy, humor, love and adventure in the hills of North Georgia.

Chapter 13
The Rest of the Story

February 1989

At the beauty shop, Arreda came in to have her hair done and to tell what happened after the silent movie was made.

"We all went to see *The Raiding Parson*. The Klan members showed it at the local meeting houses, at schools, and churches. I saw it at the Tallapoosa theater. The most people who ever attended a showing at that theater was there opening night. There were hundreds."

"I watched almost all of the movie, but when they started to show the scene where Alice Stewart got shot, I had to leave the auditorium. I couldn't take it. I went out in the lobby and waited for my friends to come out when it was over. I think the movie went bankrupt because the people who knew Alice just didn't want to see it."

As Arreda started toward the back of the beauty shop with Trisha to get her hair washed, she said, "Oh, I almost forgot. I brought you something." She handed Trisha a folder and said, "Here's a picture of me as a girl standing in a cotton field. I also brought you a lot of old newspaper clippings about Draketown. My daddy saved the newspapers in a trunk. I got those out and clipped everything there was about what happened to Alice."

"I'm so glad you brought these. I love this photo and will read all this later."

As Trisha washed Arreda's hair she continued telling about the events in Draketown.

"In those years after Alice's death, a lot of things changed—all over. I married five years after her death—when I was sixteen. But I will always remember those years especially the good times . . .

Filed in the Haralson County Courthouse, True Bill #64 This Dec. 31st 1930

Each of the accused who went to trial at the consecutive court terms were found not guilty because of irrefutable alibis. These consecutive trials were held at the appointed court sessions either in January or August: Charles "Pete" Barber in August of 1925; Owen Hendrix in January of 1926; Tate Gather in August of 1926; and Hubert Hendrix in January 1927. Ben Cash went to trial in August 1927.

True Bill #64 which began in the January Term, 1925—Murder of Mrs. Robert Stewart. Results:

The Solicitor General having stated in court that he does not have sufficient evidence to convict the defendants in this case upon motion the same is hereby **Nolle Prossed**. Price Edwards, J. S. (illegible)

Nolle Prossed is the Latin legal term for "we no longer prosecute," a declaration made to the judge by a prosecutor in a criminal case either before or during trial, meaning the case against the defendant(s) is being dropped.

The Clyde Barber Family

The last four years had gone well; then, Telma died. She took sick and was too old to fight the influenza. She was gone in two weeks. Now what to do? Janice, now eleven, dropped out of school to take care of Junior, who was now four.

When Johnny came home from school with homework, she tutored him since she had just finished the fifth grade last year. But the following year, they studied the work for the sixth grade together.

Janice told Johnny, "You pay close attention to your teacher so you can tell me her exact instruction each day when you get home."

During the day, Janice took care of Junior who was five now, and studied with Johnny while Clyde farmed during the day and did the cooking in the evenings.

The next year, all three Barber children were in school; when Junior started first grade, Janice started back and was placed in the same grade as Johnny. She was only a year behind, but could keep up. They had learned how to make do. Clyde had made a life without transporting whisky.

Toby and Mollie Barber

Though they were hard working and frugal, every winter, the Howards were out of money and food. Toby and Mollie formed a plan to survive. In the spring and summer they would plant and harvest then can and preserve. In the winter, Toby journeyed into Polk County and stayed a month. There he worked at a relative's still and made enough money to carry them over until next spring. When he came back to his family, he had a roll of money for the fruit jar, enough to do through the winter months. Thus became the pattern until the last child was grown and had left home.

Dr. William and Mrs. Jesse Hogue

After Jesse Hogue testified in court, people said they did not know how she got through it, but guessed her prayer on the stand gave her the strength. After she saw Alice shot, after Alice died, and after she had to testify in court, Jesse was emotionally drained. Dr. Hogue had to get her away from Draketown. They moved to Villa Rica about six months after the first court trial. There she focused on her son and two daughter. Over time she gradually became active in this community as she had been in Draketown.

Dr. William Hogue had a long career in Villa Rica and generations later residents remember him with great respect.

Jackson & Melviney Bingham and Family

Four years after Alice Stewart died, there were great changes in the Bingham family. Alpha and Omega were sixty-five-years-old when they died within six months of each other. Omega, who went first, had come down with dropsy: excess fluid in her ankles, legs, and joints. When she could not get around and with a weak heart from having the influenza in 1918, she gave up and would not get out of bed. She developed pneumonia and passed away within twenty-four hours.

Alpha said she had no reason to live after that. One morning, she did not get up. When Melviney found her, she was laying quiet, pale, and at peace. She was worn out taking care of her twin sister. Since they were both spinsters, the only family they had was each other and Jackson's family.

"If Alpha had gone first, Omega would not have lasted long without her," everyone at Alpha's funeral said, "They were Alpha and Omega—the beginning and the ending of their own little family; they had been close those sixty-five years. When Omega—the ending went first, that left the beginning alone, but not for long."

Melviney, who had taken up the extra activities of caring for the twins while they were sick, became stressed and overworked. Caring for them and the usual duties of a large family wore her down. After the twins passed, their room had to be cleaned and cleared out. She had spent all day going through their keepsakes and going through old pictures. There was one large stack made to keep, one pile to give away, and one pile to discard.

Late in the evening after supper, she went to the front room where Jackson was smoking his pipe and reading the newspaper. She collapsed in the overstuffed side chair and fell asleep. Jackson glanced over and decided not to disturb her as she looked so tired.

When he finished his newspaper, he went over to tell her it was time to come to bed; he roused her and said, "this is all too much for you. We are going to look for a smaller place to rent."

Bud had plans to marry a young lady, Miss Posey Singley, who taught at the Draketown school. So after his marriage the next spring, Jackson and Melviney, Boots and Arreda moved into a small house on the edge of Draketown. Arreda could still walk to Draketown school.

When Boots graduated, he tried to find work. He did not want to farm. He had no experience working on a farm and he did not have money to buy land. The depression years were upon them. He later went to work at the the grist mill with Bud and worked there most of his life. He always remembered Tannie fondly. They wrote to each other for a few years until she married. He married a young lady from Draketown.

Arreda married at sixteen to Johnny Denton. They moved to Hiram, Georgia and had two daughters. Arreda died in 1994 and is buried near in Powder Springs, Georgia.

Reverend Robert Stewart, Mattie, Tannie and Lorene

After the demise of the Milo Moving Picture Company, Robert Stewart returned to being an itinerate pastor. His family was assigned to The Green Circuit in the

Lorene, Robert, & Mattie
Courtesy Elaine Gregory

Athens District until 1929. In March, 1929 they were assigned to Sylvan Hills in Atlanta.

Oct. 4, 1930, The Atlanta Constitution, Incendiarism Probed in Stewart Blaze: Pastor Charges Fire at His Home Was Work of Liquor Runners

Officials of the fire department Friday launched an investigation into the cause of a fire which shortly after midnight Thursday damaged the 1620 Evans Drive home of the Reverend Robert Stewart, pastor of the Sylvan Hills Methodist Church. Afterward, the minister had charged the fire was the work of liquor runners he had been attacking from his pulpit.

The minister reported he believed the fire may have been an aftermath of a feud between himself and Haralson County bootleggers, who were accused of slaying his first wife while Stewart was pastor of a church at Draketown about six years ago.

Sheriff G. B. Richards, of Haralson County, said Friday afternoon he recalled the slaying of Mrs. Stewart and that several alleged liquor dealers were accused of the murder, tried and acquitted. Sheriff Richards said the pastor left Draketown shortly after the slaying and as far as he knew the enmity between Mr. Stewart and the alleged liquor runners no longer existed.

The fire Thursday night badly damaged the frame dwelling on Evans

L-R Tannie, Lorene
Courtesy Hazel Barnes

Mattie, Tannie & Emma Wood, Mattie's cousin
Courtesy Hazel Barnes

Drive. Secretary Carlton, of the board of firemasters, said fire department reports of the blaze attributed it to flying sparks from an undetermined source, but that apparently there had been no cause to suspect incendiarism. In view of the pastor's charges, however, Secretary Carlton said the matter would be investigated fully.

Obituary of Reverend Robert John Stewart

North Georgia Methodism lost one of its most consecrated ministers on Sunday, November 6, 1949 when "Brother Bob" Stewart departed for his eternal home. Robert Stewart, 61, pastor of the South Lincoln Methodist circuit, died early today at the Washington, Georgia, hospital after a month's illness. He was born on October 4, 1887 in White County, Georgia. The call of God to preach came to him when just a boy and he began his ministry at the age of 18.

Brother Bob preached for 44 years for the Methodist Church. He served the following charges: Lumpkin Mission, Dawsonville, Whitesburg, Armuchee, Draketown, Green Circuit, Sylvan Hills, South Bend, Center Hill, Palmetto Circuit, Glenn Circuit, Fuller's Circuit, Kensington, Lula and South Lincoln in which he was laboring for the fifth year.

He first married Wildie Adams, deceased, and to this union were two daughters, Mrs. Tom Butler and Mrs. Robert Butler. In 1925 he married Mattie Wood, who during these 24 years has been a great help and inspiration. Besides his wife, he is also survived by his two daughters, two sons-in-law, five grandchildren, two brothers, John and William, and one sister, Mrs. Steve Harbin of Conway, South Carolina.

Robert Stewart was a fearless evangel of God and fought social evils wherever he found them. Many souls were won into the Kingdom, and many youth challenged to enter full-time Christian service through his ministry. He loved to tell the story of Jesus and His love.

Neither Tannie nor Lorene ever got over losing their mother. At a young age, Tannie went to visit her Grandmother Adams in north Georgia. She chose to live there with her grandmother. In pursuing her musical gift, she began to play in a band with two young men—and stayed. She married in 1927, at age 20 to Thomas Butler.

Fifteen-year-old Lorene went to visit Tannie and saw what a nice comfortable life she had. She was convinced that she would be happier married and away from her very religious, strict step-mother, Mattie. She soon married Tannie's brother-in-law, Robert Butler in 1934 when she was sixteen. The two young couples lived in the same town and remained in close contact; their children were double-first cousins. Tannie had two sons; Lorene had a son and two daughters.

Tannie's was not a happy life, but she loved her sons who were loving and loyal to her and took care of her in her later years.

Lorene was a loving mother and wife and was especially drawn to young people as she said to her family many times, "I never really had a childhood. I saw my mother killed, lived under strict religious discipline, and married so young."

Lorene Stewart Butler, Courtesy Hazel Barnes

Lorene's granddaughter by her son, Bill Butler, is Julie. Julie was born on her grandmother, Alice Stewart's, birthday, May 10th. Julie has traveled the world, living in Costa Rica and teaching English in Japan and Argentina. Lorene told Julie she was a lot like her mother—Julie's grandmother, Alice. As a birthday present for Julie in 1994, Lorene called her in Japan and told her the entire story, as she remembered it and as it was told to her by the older folk about what happened to Alice "Wildie" Adams Stewart.

Life is like a river, sometimes turbulent, sometimes calm and peaceful; you cannot touch the same water twice because the flow that has passed will never come this way again. Enjoy every moment and make the most of your life.

Julie Colombini, Alice's great-granddaughter
Courtesy Hazel Barnes

BIBLIOGRAPHY

The Boll Weevil Song <http://ingeb.org/songs/odebollw.html>

Introduction and Prologue: 2004, *A Historical Sketch of Draketown,* by Peggy Kimball October: http://www.rootsweb.ancestry.com/-gahchs/stories/Draketown.html. Mike Campbell, Draketown; Wendell Rush, Draketown; John Reeves, Jr., Draketown; Anita Reeves, Draketown; Robert Nix, Athens, GA; Cecil Dewberry, Bremen, GA; Gene Cohran, Draketown; James Carden, Tallapoosa, GA.; Martha Goldin Church, Draketown, Judy Reeves Hoffman, Draketown, Kenny and Barbara Johnson, Draketown; and Maggie Edwards, Draketown.

Chapter 1 New Itinerate Preacher
Interview with Stewart family members, Hazel Barnes, Betty Sue Butler, Julie Colombini and Novaleen Butler.
July 20, 1922, "Preacher-Defiant. Continues Fight on Moonshiners, Despite Grim Warning," *The Gettysburg Times Gettysburg, Pennsylvania.*
ancestry.com and newspapers.com.

Chapter 2 Bad Times
Interview with: Patsy Bollen and Gene Cohran.
1995, *Haralson Heritage*, Dr. Allen Wilburn, Brentwood Christian Press.
1909, Practical Music Reader No. 1, Open the Pearly Gate page 117. S. J. Oslin, J. S. Torbett. Published by Ruebush-Kieffer Co. Dayton, Virginia. From the collection of Reverend Robert Stewart, Courtesy Hazel Butler.

Chapter 3 Why Stewart Hates Alcohol
Interviews with: Mike Campbell, Draketown; Wendell Rush, Draketown; Marcia Otwell, South Carolina; Daniel Swofford, Douglasville, GA; John Reeves, Jr., Drake-

town; Anita Reeves, Draketown; Robert Nix, Athens, GA; Cecil Dewberry, Bremen, GA; Gene Cohran, Draketown; James Carden, Tallapoosa, GA.

Chapter 4 Warfare on Bootleggers
Interviews with: Mike Campbell, Draketown; Wendell Rush, Draketown; John Reeves, Jr., Draketown; Anita Reeves, Draketown; Robert Nix, Athens, GA; Cecil Dewberry, Bremen, GA; Gene Cohran, Draketown; James Carden, Tallapoosa, GA.; Martha Goldin Church; and Judy Reeves Hoffman.

Chapter 5 Spirits Collide
November 21, 1924, *The Atlanta Constitution,* "Dramatic Story of Wife's Death Told by Pastor."
Interview with Gene Cohran.

Chapter 6 Two Night-Riders Wounded
Interview with Hazel Barnes, daughter of Lorene Stewart Butler, and Julie Butler Colombini, granddaughter of Lorene Stewart Butler.
November 1924, *The Haralson County Tribune.*

Chapter 7 Posse
November 15, 1924, "Pastor's Wife Fatally Shot by Rum Runners Who Made Attempt to Abduct Her Husband," *The Atlanta Constitution.*
November 15, 1924, "Draketown Woman Is Brought to Atlanta Hospital, Where Little Hope for Recovery Is Held. *The Atlanta Constitution*, page 1.
November 15, 1924, "Mrs. Stewart Dies at Hospital Here," *The Atlanta Constitution,* page 1 and 4.
November 16, 1924, "2 More Arrested in Murder of Pastor's Wife," *The Atlanta Constitution,* page 1 and 4.
November 17, 1924, "Woman's Slayers Sought in Hills," *The Atlanta Constitution.*
November 18, 1924, "Ten Men are Held in Woman's Death," *The Atlanta Constitution.*
November 20, 1924, "Ten Suspects Jailed for Shooting Pastor's Wife," *Haralson County Tribune.*
November 20, 1924, "8 to Face Court in Stewart Death," *The Atlanta Constitution.*

November 21, 1924. "Five Suspects in Slaying of Pastor's Wife are held for Grand Jury on Murder Charges," *The Atlanta Constitution*, pages 1, 4 and 7.

Chapter 8 The Community and State Reacts

Interview with Barry Boyd, grandson of Dr. and Mrs. W. L. Hogue.

November 17, 1924, "Mrs. Stewart's Death Eulogized by Dr. Dempsey," *The Atlanta Constitution*.

November 1924, "Klan Passes Resolution," *The Haralson County Tribune*.

November 21, 1924, "Baptist Deplore Killing of Woman as Crime Climax, *The Atlanta Constitution,* page 1 and 2.

November 21, 1924, "Georgia Woman's Christian Temperance Union, Law Enforcement Memorial Services," *The Atlanta Constitution*.

November 24, 1924, ""Klansmen Make Impressive Visit to Draketown Pastor," *The Atlanta Constitution*.

November 27, 1924, "Klansmen Make Impressive Visit to Draketown Pastor," *Haralson County Tribune*.

November 28, 1924, "Georgia Woman's Christian Temperance Union, President Sends New Year's Message," *The Atlanta Constitution*.

November 29, 1924, "North Georgia Methodists Honor Mrs. Stewart Sunday," *The Atlanta Constitution*.

December 11, 1924, *"Tallapoosa* W. C. T. U. Makes a Strong Stand For Law Enforcement," *The Haralson County Tribune*.

December 4, 1924, "A Proclamation," *The Haralson County Tribune*.

January 11, 1925, "Mrs. Nunn Leads Movement For Memorial to Mrs. Stewart," *The Atlanta Constitution*.

Chapter 9 Lies and Alibis

November 16, 1924, "Barber Brothers Held as Wounded Woman Succumbs." Atlanta Constitution,

November 16, 1924, "2 More Arrested in Murder of Pastor's Wife," *The Atlanta Constitution*.

November 27, 1924, "Five Suspects Held Without Bail in Stewart Slaying Case," *Haralson County Tribune*.

December 11, 1924, "Sheriff and Posse Destroy Nine Giant Stills Saturday; 4 Men

are Captured in Raid," *The Haralson County Tribune*.
December 1924, "Sheriff and Posse Destroy Nine Giant Stills Saturday; 4 Men are Captured in Raid," *Haralson County Tribune*.
January 21, 1925, "Grand Jury Considers Stewart Case Wednesday Indictments Are Sought," *The Atlanta Constitution*.
January 30, 1925, "Stewart Case Set for Next Monday," *The Atlanta Constitution*.
February 1, 1925, "Trial at Buchanan of Stewart Case," *The Atlanta Constitution*.
February 2, 1925, "Five Face Trial for Slaying Wife of Parson Raider," *The Anniston Star*, (Anniston, Alabama).
February 3, 1925, "Men Identified in Stewart Case," *The Atlanta Constitution*, p. 5.
February 4, 1925, "Stewart Case Goes to Jury, Verdict Soon," *The Atlanta Constitution*, page 1.
February 5, 1925, "One Acquitted in Slaying of Parson's Wife," *The Anniston Star*.
February 5, 1925, "Hendrix Freed in Stewart Case," The Atlanta Constitution

Chapter 10 Thunderball Over Draketown

May 28, 1925, "Monument to be Unveiled Sunday at Draketown," *The Bremen Gateway*.
May 31, 1925, "Monument to Martyr Woman," *The Atlanta Constitution*.
June 1, 1925, "Stewart Shaft Unveiled Sunday, *The Atlanta Constitution*, page 1 & 3.
June 1, 1925, "Monument to Slain Woman is Unveiled," *The Anniston Star*, page 1.
June 4, 1925, "Stewart Shaft Unveiled Sunday At Draketown," *The Bremen Gateway*, page 1.

Chapter 11 Moonshiners Without a Still

November 6, (illegible) 1924, "An Example of Pastor's Work in Liquor Raids," *The Rockmart News*.
February 3, 1925, "Four More Jailed in Slaying of Pastor's Wife, Seven Others Sought," *The Atlanta Constitution* and *The Anniston Star*, pages 1 and 5.
February 4, 1925, "Two Additional Warrants Issued in Stewart Case," *The Anniston Star*, page 1.
March 26, 1925, "3 New Arrests in Slaying of Parson's Wife," The Anniston Star, pages 1 and 3.
March 27, 1925, "Two More are Arrested as Mob Members, Four Others Sought,"

The Anniston Star, p. 1.
August 14, 1925, "Night-Riders Flog Pastor Near Scene of Stewart Killing," *The Atlanta Constitution.* Page 1.
August 14, 1925, "Revenge Seen in Whipping of Minister," *The Anniston Star*.
August 15, 1925, "Reverend Holmes, Baptist Minister, Assaulted in Tallapoosa, Ga." *The Gaffney Ledger* (Gaffney, South Carolina).
January 9, 1926, "Raiding Parson is Fired as Officer," *The Gaffney Ledger*.

Chapter 12 A Silent Movie—*The Raiding Parson*
Interview with Joe Mosley, Bremen, GA; documents from the J. W. Mozley collection: pages 1-32.
May 27, 1926, "Stewart Tragedy Put On Screen By Local People," *The Atlanta Constitution*.
May 27, 1926, "Anniston Boy Takes Part in Murder Film," *The Anniston Star,* p. 8.
June 29, 1926, "Raiding Parson Shows to Crowd at Auditorium," *The Atlanta Constitution*.

Chapter 13 The Rest of the Story Oct. 4, 1930, "Incendiarism Probed in Stewart Blaze," *The Atlanta Constitution*.
A collection of Stewart Family History with artifacts and photos; Hazel Barnes, Betty Butler, Novaleen Butler, Julie Butler Colombini.

Other Documentation

History
October 2004, *A Historical Sketch of Draketown,* by Peggy Kimball, <http://www.rootsweb.ancestry.com/~gahchs/stories/Draketown.html>
1991, *Haralson County, Georgia; A Resource Guide for the Teaching of Social Studies in Haralson County, GA,* Chapter Seven "Historical Markers and Monuments," by R. Allen Wilburn.

Magazine
2004, Draketown's "82-year-old Murder Mystery; The Unsolved Slaying of Alice Stewart," *The Tallapoosa Journal, The Haralson Gateway-Beacon*.
Autumn 2005, "Murder, Moonshine, Ku Klux Klan," R. Allen Wilburn, *Georgia*

Backroads, page 24-26.

March/April 2014, *"Murder in Draketown: 90 Years later - 'the Raiding Parson's' Tale Lives On,"* by Ken Denney, *West Georgia Living*, pgs. 42- 45.

Pamphlet

1941, *Alcohol—A Deadly Necrotic* by George P. Lamar, father of Patricia Lamar Mullinax, coauthor.

Publications

1995, Haralson Heritage, Chapter Twelve - A Martyr for Law and Order, Dr. Allen Wilburn, Brentwood Christian Press.

Songs

Adaptation of: *The Boll Weevil Song*: <http://ingeb.org/songs/odebollw.html>

Cotton Eyed Joe: <https://en.wikipedia.org/wiki/Cotton-Eyed_Joe>

About the Authors

Elaine Bolden Bailey has lived in Douglas County, Georgia since 1970, earned a B. S. degree in Ed. from the U. of W. Georgia, and retired from W. Georgia Technical College as an Adult Education Instructor. Elaine and her husband, John, have two children, a son-in-law, and two grandchildren.

Elaine's interests are writing, history, and genealogy. She has written two poetry books, Pompadour and Pearls: A Patchwork of Poetry in 1991, Buttermilk Clouds in 1995; Explosion in Villa Rica, non-fictional history in 2010; Tracks, a historical novel in 2011; and has collaborated with her husband in 2014 for his book, History of Dark Corner Campbell County, Georgia.

Patricia Lamar Mullinax was born in Carroll Co. and has lived there all her life. She has one grown son, Todd Parrish. Trisha sold real estate and worked as a beautician for over twenty years in Villa Rica, Georgia. Trisha and her husband, Steve Mullinax, are both Civil War historians and accomplished relic hunters, hunting over many Confederate battlegrounds in the Southeastern United States. Together, they published two books: Confederate Belt Buckles and Plates in August of 1999 and In the Line of Fire in 2006.

Trisha had a life long attraction to this Draketown story, to the community, and to the secrets that lie waiting to be uncovered. When she began the research, she made a startling discovery. She is a direct descendant of Dr. W. F. Goldin, one of the early pioneers in Draketown. Trisha's great-grandmother, Jane, who married Ruben Reid, is Dr. W. F. Goldin's sister.

Draketown Tragedy

www.ingramcontent.com/pod-product-compliance
Lightning Source LLC
Chambersburg PA
CBHW080338170426
43194CB00014B/2611